Prolog Programming and Applications

W.D. Burnham
and
A.R. Hall

MACMILLAN

First published 1985

Published by
MACMILLAN EDUCATION LTD
Houndmills, Basingstoke, Hampshire RG21 2XS
and London
Companies and representatives
throughout the world

Typeset by TecSet Ltd, Sutton, Surrey
Printed in Great Britain by
Camelot Press Ltd,
Southampton

ISBN 0-333-39159-4

Contents

Preface   *viii*
Acknowledgements   *xi*

1 Introducing the Language   **1**
  1.1   Writing assertive statements   1
  1.2   Syntax requirements   2
  1.3   More complex statements   3
  1.4   Exercise 1   4
  1.5   Formulating rules   4
  1.6   Exercise 2   6
  1.7   Building and questioning a knowledge
          base   7
  1.8   Introducing rules to the knowledge base   11
  1.9   Exercise 3   12
  1.10 Summary of syntax rules   12
  1.11 Solutions to exercises   14
  1.12 Practical projects   16

2 The Structure of the Language   **17**
  2.1   Predicates and arguments   17
  2.2   The idea of goals in Prolog   18
  2.3   Structures within Prolog clauses   19
  2.4   Exercise 4   22
  2.5   The 'blank' variable   22
  2.6   Search and pattern matching   24
  2.7   Exercise 5   28
  2.8   Diagrammatic representation of
          backtracking   28
  2.9   Solutions to exercises   29

**3 Arithmetic, the "Cut" Symbol, and
    Recursion**   **31**
  3.1   Arithmetic   31
  3.2   Exercise 6   35
  3.3   The "cut" symbol   35

	3.4	Exercise 7	37
	3.5	Recursion in Prolog	37
	3.6	Exercise 8	41
	3.7	Solutions to exercises	42

4 Lists and Complex Structures **45**

	4.1	Lists in Prolog	45
	4.2	The structure of lists	45
	4.3	Special list notation	46
	4.4	Using lists and list notation	47
	4.5	Exercise 9	47
	4.6	Incorporating more complex data structures in lists	48
	4.7	Manipulating the contents of lists	49
	4.8	Exercise 10	51
	4.9	Solutions to exercises	52

5 Interactive Programming using Prolog **53**

	5.1	Input of information to the program	53
	5.2	Output of information to the user	54
	5.3	Exercise 11	57
	5.4	Some more system predicates	57
	5.5	Exercise 12	60
	5.6	Getting Prolog to 'learn'	61
	5.7	Generating multiple solutions inside the program	63
	5.8	Solutions to exercises	66

6 More Advanced Programming Tools **68**

	6.1	Predicates for input and output	68
	6.2	Modifying the database	72
	6.3	Meta logical predicates	74
	6.4	Performing logical tests	76
	6.5	Operators	77
	6.6	The Prolog high-level grammar syntax	80

7 The Debugging Facility **83**

	7.1	The box model	83
	7.2	The debugging predicates	85

8 Case Studies **90**

Contents

Appendix 1: Prolog-1 (Version 2)   101

Appendix 2: Quintus Prolog (Version 1.2)   106

Appendix 3: A List of ASCII Characters and
*   their Codes*   111

Index   113

Preface

Prolog: an introduction to the language

Since 1980, world-wide interest in the fields of Artificial Intelligence, Knowledge Processing and Expert Systems has increased. The spread of ideas associated with these subjects has been furthered by the announcement of the Japanese Fifth Generation Computing initiative, the response to that in the United States, the production in the U.K. of the Alvey report on Information Technology and European responses such as the ESPRIT program. The situation now is that most of those people who are seriously involved in computing — whether as academics, professional practitioners or students — have some acquaintance with the concepts associated with Expert or Knowledge Based Systems.

In order to use the ideas, it has been necessary to find new ways of communicating our requirements to computer systems. Two languages in particular have emerged as the vehicles for developing and implementing Expert Systems — Prolog and LISP.

Both languages have attracted a dedicated user group because they offer a wider range of expression to the programmer than do other established languages. In brief, both languages allow, in their different ways, for the symbolic representation of some parts of human knowledge and reasoning.

Although they have some common characteristics, Prolog and LISP have different histories and, at the time of writing, there is a notable contrast in the way in which the languages have been implemented. LISP is the older language by more than a decade and the original development is credited to John McCarthy. LISP has been available as a usable language since the early sixties. Being essentially a simple and 'open' language, the strength of LISP is that its structure has allowed the development of beautifully engineered programming environments, examples of these being ZETALISP from MIT and INTERLISP-D from Xerox PARC. Running on dedicated machines with micro-coding capability (for example, Symbolics, Xerox 1108, LM1 lambda) these environments undoubtedly represent the most sophisticated programming tools available to us.

Prolog has a somewhat different history, having originated in Europe on the basis of work done by Alain Colmerauer and team at the University of Marseilles. Since the mid seventies much of the definitive development work on Prolog has been carried out in the U.K.

Up until a couple of years ago, LISP was regarded as the American Artificial Intelligence language and Prolog that of Europe. That situation is now changing and Prolog is gaining acceptance in the U.S.A. at the same time that powerful LISP environments are becoming extensively used in Europe.

Although there are as yet no specialised Prolog implementations that match the sophistication of the best LISP environments, it is only a matter of time before they are produced. Japan has selected Prolog as the base language for the Fifth Generation Programme and have stated that a primary objective is the development of a dedicated Prolog machine. A team at Berkeley University is currently working on the development of a similar system and there is work in that direction being carried out at Imperial College, London.

There are now a number of implementations of Prolog; some are excellent, others weak to the point of being little more than refined toys. The number of different 'dialects' means that there may be cases where examples used in this book will need to be restated to suit a different Prolog environment. The examples and test programs were constructed on the following systems, with minor changes in syntax.

The DEC-10 system running University of Edinburgh Prolog (Warren, Pereira, Byrd).
The SUN-2 system running Quintus Prolog (Artificial Intelligence Ltd).
The IBM PC system running Prolog-1 (Expert Systems Ltd).

About the book

Our intention has been to produce a reference book which will allow students of the Prolog language to reach a good standard of proficiency in a fairly short period of time. As with all programming languages, there is a point at which the programmer must take over control of the learning process and build upon a basis of understanding in order to obtain the results he or she wants from the language. This is particularly true of Prolog because there are few constraints upon the power of expression that the language offers. It is possible to teach someone the syntax of the language but it is not entirely possible to teach people to use it productively — that comes with experience and motivation.

Although there is a considerable amount of theory and academic knowledge which is appropriate to the advanced study of Prolog, we have made a conscious decision to exclude most of it from this book. Much of it is treated in *Programming in Prolog* (Clocksin and Mellish; Springer-Verlag), and the reader is recommended to pass on to that text after assimilating this one.

Throughout the book, we have concentrated on obtaining practical results from the use of Prolog — thus the examples used tend to illustrate how a particular process can be implemented in Prolog and the reader is then (we hope) able to adapt the technique to his or her own requirements. By the time you have finished reading the book we very much hope that you will share our opinion that Prolog is a fascinating and delightful language to use, concealing great depth and power behind its apparent simplicity.

Acknowledgements

The authors take great pleasure in expressing their thanks and appreciation to the following groups and individuals, without whom the book could not have been written:

Friends and colleagues at the Faculty of Engineering, Polytechnic of the South Bank. In particular John Hempstead, Chris Clare, Jack Dwyer, and Denbigh Gabbitas.
David Butler and the staff of Artificial Intelligence Ltd for encouragement, help and computing facilities.
Alex Goodall and the staff of Expert Systems International Ltd for their friendly co-operation.
The British Technology Group for their co-operation.
Lawrence Byrd and David Warren of the Quintus Corporation for their expertise and incisive comment.

1 Introducing the Language

If you are familiar with languages such as Cobol, Pascal or Algol, it may well be that you will find Prolog a little elusive at first. One reason for this is that Prolog does not have to execute a series of procedural steps; it is a declarative language which allows the programmer to make direct statements and assertions about objects and relationships. Furthermore, when writing a Prolog program, the programmer uses the same structure and syntax to create the database which the system will use. Since Prolog is often associated with Expert and Knowledge Based Systems, the database is sometimes referred to as the 'knowledge base'. When a Prolog program has been written, and compiled or interpreted, it is immediately available for questioning — there is an interactive mechanism built into the language which means that no special routines need be programmed to allow the program to be interrogated from the terminal.

Once the initial adjustment to the nature of the language has been made, you will find Prolog to be a powerful and sympathetic language which allows the simple development of systems that would be difficult to program in a procedural language.

The main purpose of this book is to enable the reader to make a successful start with Prolog and to use it in a productive manner. For that reason the philosophical basis of the language and the latest research in its applications are not discussed. However, for those who may be interested in pursuing the matter further, the language is derived from predicate calculus, a discipline of formal logic which in general terms is concerned with the provability of statements, and it is recommended that serious study of the theoretical aspects of the language should begin with an understanding of that discipline.

1.1 Writing assertive statements

An assertion (or proposition) is a statement about something which may be true or untrue and as human beings we have the ability to make assertions about anything (the truth of them is a different matter however). Thus, the following are all assertions, some true, some not

John is a programmer
Bob and Carol are married to each other

The Prime Minister is charming
The Earth is flat
Armageddon is nigh

It is easy to program such assertions in Prolog, and once programmed they
form part of the knowledge base of the program. We discuss how the knowledge
base can be accessed in section 1.7, but first we will examine how assertions
such as the ones above may be programmed.

If we take a very simple example, "John is a programmer", and wish to
represent that fact in our knowledge base (perhaps for a personnel registration
system), we simply write

programmer (john).

Note that the category, programmer, is placed first and the subject of the
assertion is bracketed and placed after it. The reason for adopting this con-
vention will become clear as you learn more about the language.

Here are some more simple assertions

boy (jim).
saint (nicholas).
politician (joseph).
traitor (judas).
prime_minister (wilson).
prime_minister (thatcher).

There is one important point that needs to be emphasised from the outset:
the programmer has complete control over the truth and relevance of the assertions made. There is no mechanism that can check for or correct inconsistent
statements such as

woman (pope_john).

1.2 Syntax requirements

Although the syntax requirements for Prolog are generally straightforward and
easy to learn, there are certain rules that need to be observed. Note the following

(i) No capital letters are used. In Prolog, capitals have a special significance
(see section 1.5). When programming assertions at the moment use lower
case letters only.
(ii) The two parts of the statement (known as the predicate and the arguments)
are separated from each other by brackets. The arguments are bracketed.

(iii) Each assertion must terminate with a full stop. Common sense tells us that Prolog must have some way of knowing when an assertion is complete and the full stop provides that.

(iv) You will notice that where a predicate is composed of more than one word (for example, **prime minister**), then when it is written in the assertion the words are separated by the underline character. The reason for this is that both obvious ways of separating two words, that is using a hyphen or a space, are inadmissible in Prolog. Although in general terms spaces are ignored in Prolog syntax, they are not permitted to appear in predicates or arguments, which require an unbroken string of characters. The hyphen command cannot be used as it is reserved for another use (see chapter 3). Remember, therefore, to separate with the underline character, for example

> **first_class**
> **northern_dancer**
> **john_smith**

1.3 More complex statements

The examples given in section 1.1 are assertions which express the relationship "is" about a single subject. For instance, the assertion **programmer (john)** can be translated to "john is a programmer". However, it is possible to program assertions about more complex relationships between two or more objects or individuals. Suppose we wish to extend our information about john the programmer to include a reference to his employer, Software plc. We can make the assertion

> **employs (software_p_l_c, john).**

We have now established the relation of employment between two separate entities. Once more, however, it is essential to stress that *the programmer is in control of the meaning of the assertion and its accuracy*. We have chosen to represent the assertion "Software plc employs John" in the most straightforward way, but the relationship could have been expressed just as well by stating

> **employer (john, software_p_l_c).**

that is, "the employer of John is Software plc" — it depends entirely on how the programmer wishes to represent assertions. Note how the order in which the arguments of the clause are written is flexible and can be altered to give a more precise meaning to the assertion.

Here are some more assertions which represent relationships between two or more entities

> **father (john, michael).**   "the father of John is Michael"

married (jack, mavis).   "Jack and Mavis are a married couple"
parents (george, jack, mavis).   "the parents of George are Jack and Mavis"
pet (tommy, angela, bill).   "Tommy is the pet of Angela and Bill"

Note that when there are two or more arguments referred to in the assertion they must be separated by a comma. Thus the assertion

father (john michael).

is incorrectly stated because the comma has not been inserted.

1.4 Exercise 1

Write these assertions as Prolog statements.

  (i) "Joey is a canary"
 (ii) "the father of Mary is Paul"
(iii) "the sire of Nijinsky is Northern Dancer"
(iv) "the Father of John is Michael" and "the father of Jane is Michael"
    (Here there are two separate statements but their meanings should be compatible.)
 (v) "John, Paul, George and Ringo were the Beatles"

1.5 Formulating rules

Although it is essential to be able to state assertions in the way described, the power of Prolog becomes greatly extended when rules are formulated, for it is rules which allow the inference mechanism of the language to operate. We stated earlier that capital letters have a special significance in Prolog — they are used to express *variables*.

When we move from making assertions to formulating rules we are effectively moving from the specific to the general and we need, therefore, to utilise a notation that allows us to represent variables. There is a significant difference between the statements "John is a programmer" and "a person who is skilled in one or more computer languages and is employed in that capacity is a programmer". The former establishes an item of information about one person whereas the latter offers us a workable definition of programmer into which we may fit a large number of individuals. Moreover, we know that any individual who is both skilled in a language and employed in that capacity is a programmer according to our requirements. The example is fairly trivial but the underlying concept is most important.

Look at a few examples of simple rules. They will allow us to discuss the important ideas associated with each rule formulation.

(i) **computer_technician (X):-programmer (X).**
(ii) **programmer (X):-skilled_in_prolog (X), employed (X).**
(iii) **man (X) :- male (X), adult (X).**
(iv) **boy (X) :- male (X), child (X).**
(v) **married (X, Y) :- wife (X, Y).**
or **married (X, Y) :- husband (Y, X).**

To an experienced Prolog programmer the above rules are simple and straight-forward. Nonetheless, there are a number of very important points that can be learned from examining them. We will take each rule in turn and highlight what can be learned from it.

Example (i)

Here we are stating a rule about a sub-category of computer technicians: programmers. Now although all programmers are computer technicians the reverse is not the case, there are many technically skilled people in the computer industry who are not employed as programmers (for example, operators, support engineers, designers, etc.). Programmers therefore represent a subset of computer technicians and our rule states that if we can find an entity that is a programmer then we have also found an entity that is a computer technician.
Note the syntax:

(a) The variable is enclosed in brackets.
(b) The same variable appears on both sides of the rule.
(c) Although X is used as the variable in this case, anything beginning with a capital letter could have been used. For example

   computer_technician (Someone):-programmer (Someone).

(d) The two parts of the rule are separated by the inference symbol :- which for the purpose of introducing the basic language structure may be taken to mean 'if'. You should be aware however that 'if' in this context is used somewhat differently from its use in a conventional (that is, procedural) language where it will typically be associated with an 'if-then' sequence of program instructions. We do not need to concern ourselves too much with this distinction at present but it will become more significant as we introduce advanced Prolog constructs in later chapters. For example

   computer_technician (X):-programmer (X).

   can be taken to mean

   "X is a computer technician 'if' X is a programmer"

(e) The rule must terminate with a full stop.
(f) The wider category, that is, computer technician, appears on the left side
     of the :– symbol. This is important because if we were to reverse the order,
     the rule would be saying that all computer technicians are programmers
     and would be untrue.

Example (ii)

In the second example we are introducing a definition which features two components on the right-hand side of the rule, that is, a person who is skilled in a
language (in this example Prolog) *and* is employed, is a programmer. *Note the
use of the comma which means 'and' in Prolog rule formulation.*

Examples (iii) and (iv)

Here are two rules that define men and boys by finding entities that are males
and adults or children respectively.

Example (v)

Just as assertions can state relationships between one or more entities, so can
rules. Here we have two ways of defining the relationship **married** between two
individuals.
     The first rule states that "X and Y are married (to each other) 'if' the wife of
X is Y".
     The alternative rule states that "X and Y are married (to each other) 'if'
the husband of Y is X".
     A very important point to be noted is that if the two rules about marriage are
to be compatible, then the order in which the variables are written is significant.
Although it would be syntactically correct to write the two rules about marriage
shown below, they are in fact mutually exclusive in that both rules cannot be
applied to the same couple

     married (X, Y) :– wife (X, Y).
     married (X, Y) :– husband (X, Y).

That is, the statements "the wife of X is Y" and "the husband of X is Y" cannot
possibly apply to the same couple because both X and Y would each have to
represent the wife and the husband.

1.6 Exercise 2

Formulate rules to express the following

(i) A definition of a dog as a domesticated animal.

(ii) All lizards are reptiles.

(iii) Separate definitions of woman and girl which have part of the definition in common.

(iv) Two compatible rules which express the concept of one person owing money to another, using the relationships 'debtor' and 'creditor'.

1.7 Building and questioning a knowledge base

By programming a combination of assertions and rules it is possible to create a knowledge base which is then immediately available for questioning. (At this point you will need to consult appendix 1 or 2 or your User Reference Manual to commence running Prolog on your system.)

One of the most attractive features of Prolog is that you do not need to program the interactive mechanism that allows the knowledge base to be questioned — it is an intrinsic part of the language. In order to demonstrate how to question a knowledge base we will construct several simple examples.

First take an example that consists solely of assertions.

> **lizard (iguana).**
> **snake (adder).**
> **mammal (rabbit).**
> **marsupial (kangaroo).**
> **fish (shark).**

As you can see, we have some very simple assertions about living creatures. Once the appropriate action (which as we have indicated varies slightly for different systems) has been taken to enter the above program it forms the knowledge base which can then be questioned. In order to show how this is done the outputs from the Prolog system are shown on the left, and the inputs to the system by the user are shown on the right. The first interaction is a question prompt from Prolog

Prolog	*User*
?–	**lizard (iguana).**
yes	
?–	**lizard (toad).**
no	
?–	**marsupial (kangaroo).**
yes	
?–	**. . . (session ends)**

Points to note

(a) The questions posed by the user are written in the same format as the coded assertions, that is, in lower case letters terminating with a full stop.

(b) The questions posed in the first session are asking Prolog to confirm or deny (yes or no) the truth of those statements. As you can see, the user asks in turn "is it true that an iguana is a lizard"?, "is it true that a toad is a lizard"?, and "is it true that a kangaroo is a marsupial"? The answers from Prolog are "yes", "no" and "yes" respectively. They are, of course, the responses that we would expect to get by inspecting the knowledge base.

Using the same small knowledge base, we will now use a different questioning technique.

Prolog	*User*
?–	**lizard (X).**
X = iguana	**(enter carriage return)**
yes	
?–	**mammal (Mammal).**
Mammal = rabbit	
yes	
?–	**primate (X).**
no	
?–	**. . . (session ends)**

Points to note

(a) Once again, the question formats resemble the Prolog statements, but this time we have used a variable as the argument inside the brackets.

(b) We are now widening the scope of our system by asking it not to confirm or deny something, but to find some information for us. The questions asked this time are of the format "give me an example of a lizard", "give me an example of a mammal" and "give me an example of a primate". The reason why the variable has to be used is that we do not have a specific solution in mind when we ask the question; we are asking the system to provide that answer. In other words, we are asking it to find a value for the variable that makes the statement true. In this case it 'knows' of only one lizard, hence the answer **X = iguana**. Similarly, it 'knows' of only one mammal, and it 'knows' of no primates.

When questioning in this format any variable may be used. Thus we could have asked any of the following questions and received the same answer.

lizard (X).
lizard (Lizard).
lizard (A).

You will have noted from the examples so far that the knowledge base as we have written it could provide only a single answer to the questions posed. For example, the question

   ?- snake (X).

has only one possible response, that is **X = adder**, from the knowledge base provided.

However, another great strength of Prolog is the ability of the language to find all possible solutions to a given question. For instance, if we were to increase our knowledge base by adding one more assertion

   snake (cobra).

you can see that there are now two values that can provide an answer to the question

   snake (X).

The next example session shows how the user may try to extract multiple answers to the questions.

Prolog	*User*
?-	**snake (X).**
X = adder	;
X = cobra	;
no	
?-	. . . **(session ends)**

Point to note
After the question "give me an example of a snake", the user enters a semi-colon. In this situation it means, in effect, "find another solution". In the example, the system finds two solutions, adder and cobra, but when asked for a third solution it cannot find one and it therefore returns the answer, **no**.

So far, we have only questioned assertions which express very simple concepts, such as, "an adder is a snake", "a rabbit is a mammal" and so on. Now we shall add some further assertions to the knowledge base, which express the concept that some living creatures prey on others.

   prey (adder, frog).
   prey (cobra, frog).
   prey (cobra, rat).
   prey (cobra, adder).

Using the previous examples as a basis for understanding, we will conduct an example session involving the new assertions listed above.

Prolog	*User*
?–	**prey (cobra, rat).**
yes	
?–	**prey (cobra, Prey).**
Prey = frog	;
Prey = rat	;
Prey = adder	;
no	
?–	**prey (Predator, Prey).**
Predator = adder,	
Prey = frog	;
Predator = cobra,	
Prey = frog	;
Predator = cobra,	
Prey = rat	;
Predator = cobra,	
Prey = adder	;
no	
?–	**prey (Predator, frog).**
Predator = adder	;
Predator = cobra	;
no	
?–	**. . . (session ends)**

Points to note
(a) The first question is in the confirm/deny format and this time uses two arguments inside the brackets in the question "is it true that cobras prey on rats"?, to which the answer is yes.
(b) The second question **prey (cobra, Prey)**, which admittedly reads like an exhortation to a doomed sinner – is in effect saying "what do cobras prey on?" As you can see, their diet includes frogs, rats and other snakes. Note the use of the semi-colon to elicit those answers.
(c) The third question format uses two variables and is asking the system "what preys on what?" or in paraphrase "tell me about a predator and its prey". Once again the semi-colon prompts all available answers, four of them, which are given with both parts of the question answered, that is both predator and prey are identified.
(d) Finally, we reverse the earlier question format and instead of asking what cobras and adders prey on, we ask in effect "what preys on frogs?" or to put it another way "what do frogs need to watch out for?". Both types of

snake are partial to the odd frog and so both adder and cobra are returned as answers.

1.8 Introducing rules to the knowledge base

The examples in the previous section were all concerned with questioning a program comprising only assertions. All the information contained was *explicit*, in other words there was no deduction or inference involved in reaching the answers given. However, Prolog is able to carry out more sophisticated processes which do require the use of inference in order to reach conclusions. To activate the inference mechanism of the language it is necessary to introduce rules to the knowledge base. We will now add a new rule to the small knowledge base already used

carnivore (X) :- prey (X, Y).

The above rule states that for **X** to be a carnivorous creature, **X** must prey on **Y**. In this instance the identity of **Y** is not important, any creature that preys on another must be a carnivore. At present, the above rule is the only one in our knowledge base but we can use it to illustrate how the inference mechanism works.

Prolog	*User*
?-	**carnivore (X).**
X = adder	
yes	
?-	**. . . (session ends)**

Points to note
Until the last question was posed, every question that has been asked was related directly to an assertion. However, there is no assertion of the type

carnivore (. .)

in the knowledge base.

    However there is a rule which states that any creature that preys on another is a carnivore. Using that rule, it is then possible to see if there are any creatures that prey on others. Of course, in this case the assertion

prey (adder, frog).

gives that information. With the assertion *and* the rule it is possible to *infer* that, since a carnivore preys on another creature, and since an adder preys on a frog, then an adder is a carnivore. Just as we are able to match a rule with an assertion to infer a conclusion, so also is Prolog.

Although the example that has been used to illustrate this idea is a simple one, it is apparent that the mechanism is a powerful one. It is possible to build complex systems based on the ability of Prolog to infer conclusions from assertions and rules. Note also that by doing so we are taking a first step towards representing human reasoning within a computer system.

In chapter 2 there is an analysis of how Prolog goes about answering questions, and the operation of the inference mechanism. For now, we suggest that you familiarise yourself with the ideas we have discussed by doing some programming and then questioning your system. There are some exercises to help you do so.

1.9 Exercise 3

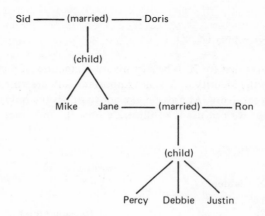

(i) Using the relationships **married**, **child**, **male** and **female**, program the family tree using assertions only.

(ii) Based on the assertions programmed in (i), add rules to the knowledge base which can define **son**, **daughter**, **mother** and **father**.

1.10 Summary of syntax rules

Using Prolog at a simple level, most of the errors that you make are likely to be because of faulty syntax. In the event of such errors Prolog will 'refuse' to use your program. Here are the main points of syntax to look out for.

(1) Incorrect use of capital letters. Remember that capitals are reserved for use as *variables* and that anything starting with a capital is taken to be a variable. For example X, Y, A, What, Something, A1, Xf are all taken to be variables.

(2) Check the use of brackets in assertions and rules. The subject of an assertion

must be bracketed as must the variable(s) associated with a rule; for example, **cat (tommy).** and **father (X)**.

(3) Assertions and rules *must* terminate with a full stop. Failure to add one accounts for a high percentage of errors when the language is first being used.

(4) Inversion of logical meaning is a common error and it is understandable why such mistakes are made. Because the programmer controls the meaning of statements, you need to be clear about what it is you are trying to say. For example, an assertion such as **person (john).** relies on a sensible interpretation based, ultimately, on familiarity with the English language — that is, "John is a person". If on the other hand, you, the programmer, choose that statement to represent "John is a nun whose real name is Sister Margaret", then Prolog cannot stop you doing so but your potential for producing systems that others can use may be rather questionable. Similarly, there is nothing to stop you programming **john (person).** , as long as the rather inane answer you get when you question the system is acceptable to you.

Much the same applies to formulating rules. As a starting point bear in mind that the dominant part of the rule appears on the *left side*. Thus the rule

   dog (X) :- carnivore (X).

is not logically correct; there are many meat-eating animals that are not dogs and you are excluding them. Also be careful of incorrectly mixing variables. The rule

   carnivore (X) :- dog (X).

is a correct logical statement because anything that is a dog must also be a carnivore. If however, you program

   carnivore (X) :- dog (Y).

achieves nothing because Prolog assumes that two different entities are being referred to. This consistency of variables applies however only within the limits of one statement. If, for instance, you program

   parent (X, Y) :- father (X), son (Y).

and then enter the question

   ?- parent (A, B).

then the problem does not arise since **A** matches with **X** and **B** matches with **Y**, so answers can be found to the question (if any exist).

(5) The comma is an important part of the language and to summarise: used inside a bracket it separates two or more subjects or variables, for example **married (fred, Y)**. Used outside the brackets it means 'and', for example

parent (X, Y) :- father (X), son (Y).

or

"X is the parent of Y if X is the father 'and' Y is the son".

(6) Here are two syntax elements that you will find useful

(a) *The semi-colon;* has already been encountered as a prompt to ask Prolog to generate an alternative answer to a question (see section 1.7). However, it may also be used in rule formulation to represent 'or'. Take a simple example. Here are two alternative definitions of parenthood

parent (X, Y) :- father (X), child (Y).
parent (X, Y) :- mother (X), child (Y).

By using 'or' we can collapse the two statements into one

parent (X, Y) :- (father (X); mother (X)), child (Y).

The 'or' statement is bracketed to ensure a complete clarity of meaning. The statement reads "X is the parent of Y if X is the father 'or' X is the mother of Y 'and' Y is a child".

(b) *The underline character* _ is used when a subject requires more than one word to describe it. You cannot use a hyphen or a space, otherwise an error will occur (as discussed earlier). It can also be used to indicate variables — see chapter 2.

1.11 Solutions to exercises

Exercise 1

  (i) **canary (joey).**
 (ii) **father (mary, paul).**
(iii) **sire (nijinsky, northern_dancer).**
 (iv) **father (john, michael).**
      father (jane, michael).
  (v) **beatles (john, paul, george, ringo).**

Note: The answers to the exercise are just suggestions. Yours may be slightly different since you control the meaning of your assertions.

Exercise 2

 (i) **dog (X) :– canine (X), domesticated (X).**
 (ii) **reptile (X) :– lizard (X).**
(iii) **woman (X) :– female (X), adult (X).**
      girl (X) :– female (X), child (X).
(iv) **owes (Debtor, Creditor) :– debtor (Debtor, Creditor).**
     owes (Debtor, Creditor) :– creditor (Creditor, Debtor).

Exercise 3

 (i) **married (sid, doris).**
     married (ron, jane).
     child (mike, sid).
     child (jane, sid).
     child (percy, ron).
     child (debbie, ron).
     child (justin, ron).
     male (sid).
     male (ron).
     male (mike).
     male (percy).
     male (justin).
     female (doris).
     female (jane).
     female (debbie).

(ii) You will notice that the assertions programmed above establish the relationship **child** between the male parent and the child. It is possible to establish the female parent using the simple rule

   child (X, Y) :– married (Z, Y), child (X, Z).

Further rules are added to establish other relationships

   son (X, Y) :– male (X), child (X, Y).
   daughter (X, Y) :– female (X), child (X, Y).
   mother (Y, X) :– female (X), child (Y, X).
   father (Y, X) :– male (X), child (Y, X).

Incidentally, there are some more family relationships that can be established by the addition of further rules, and you may care to adapt this example for practical project (i) — see section 1.12.

1.12 Practical projects

(i) Program your family tree for the previous three generations.
(ii) Design and program a small knowledge base to record details about something of interest to you. For example, if you are interested in horse racing, you could program a knowledge base recording details of the winners of classic races.

2   The Structure of the Language

In the first chapter we introduced the ideas of stating assertions, formulating rules and interrogating a program containing both assertions and rules. That chapter will have given you the opportunity to try out those basic language facilities and to gain something of a feel for the language. Our objective in this chapter will be to support that practical experience of Prolog with some of the theory and terminology associated with it. One good reason for doing this is that we shall be able to introduce more complex language facilities with the aid of a common vocabulary.

2.1 Predicates and arguments

Examine the following examples of Prolog clauses

```
man (john).
man (X) :- human (X), male (X).
married (X, Y) :- husband (Y, X); wife (X, Y).
family (X, Y, Z) :- married (X, Y), (child (Z, X); child (Z, Y)).
```

In each case the *predicate* is saying something about the subject, or subjects. The subject(s) are referred to as the *argument(s)* of the predicate. Thus we have

(i) Predicate **man** with one argument, in this particular case **john.**
(ii) Predicate **man** with one argument, defined in terms of two other predicates, **human** and **male**, each having one argument.
(iii) Predicate **married** with two arguments, defined in terms of two predicates, **husband** and **wife**, each having two arguments.
(iv) Predicate **family** with three associated arguments. Note how this is defined with reference to a previously defined rule, **married** and the new predicate **child** which has two arguments. This method of building up complexity by using previously defined clauses is a common feature of Prolog programming and is a theme to which we will return. The number of arguments associated with a predicate is known as the *arity* of that clause.

In general terms we can see that an argument associated with a predicate may be either a constant or a variable. Ultimately, of course, variables need to be *instantiated* to constants in order for a Prolog program to provide usable information. For more advanced programming it can be useful to be able to write predicates with *no* arguments, but we will discuss that idea later; at present we do not need to use it. In addition we can use the same predicate with varying arities. For example

> family (X, Y) :- husband (X), wife(Y).
> family (X, Y, Z) :- husband (X), wife (Y),
>   (child (X, Z); child (Y, Z)).

2.2 The idea of goals in Prolog

This is a concept fundamental to the use of Prolog. As a starting point, a convenient way to think of a goal is to see it as that which we actually want to achieve. For instance, if we enter the following question to a Prolog program

> ?- married (X, Y).

then our *goal* is to establish that there are values of X and Y which represent two people who are married to each other. If this is the case the goal is said to *succeed*, otherwise it is said to *fail*. If we had in our knowledge base the assertion

> married (george, ethel).

then the goal can succeed and the answer be returned (X = george, Y = ethel). The goal succeeds by matching the question against the corresponding assertion and we will examine that process in more detail in section 2.6.

It may be however, that the idea of marriage has been expressed in terms of a rule, perhaps as follows

> married (X, Y) :- husband (Y, X).

In this situation, Prolog cannot match directly with an assertion to provide a solution. For the goal in question to succeed it must, as we saw in chapter 1, resolve the rule defining **married**. To do so it needs to resolve

> husband (Y, X).

As you can see, the assertion

> husband (ethel, george).

enables this to be accomplished and the solution, as before, will be

X = george
Y = ethel

The clause **husband (Y, X)** is then said to represent a *sub-goal*, in other words, it must succeed before the *goal* **married** can succeed. Furthermore

married (X, Y).

can be said to constitute the *head* of the rule and

husband (Y, X).

constitutes the *body*.

We can extend the concept of goals succeeding by proving the success of sub-goals as follows. Consider the following knowledge base

crime (arson).
crime (robbery).
crime (murder).
tried (smith, robbery).
tried (brown, murder).
tried (jones, arson).
proven (smith, robbery).
guilty (X, Y) :- convicted (X, Y), crime (Y).
convicted (X, Y) :- tried (X, Y), proven (X, Y).

We will present our goal in the form

?- guilty (X, Y).

"who has been found guilty of what crime?".

In order to resolve this goal the rule head **guilty (X, Y)** generates the sub-goals **convicted (X, Y)** and **crime (Y)**. This is already familiar to us. However, this example introduces the important concept that a sub-goal can itself generate further sub-goals, and in this particular case the sub-goal **convicted (X, Y)** can succeed only if its own sub-goals **tried (X, Y)** and **proven (X, Y)** succeed. In fact, the goal/sub-goal hierarchy may be extended to however many levels are necessary to state a programming task. (A detailed analysis of the way in which goals succeed or fail is given in section 2.6.)

2.3 Structures within Prolog clauses

As we have seen, a Prolog clause consists, in simple terms, of predicates and associated arguments and the arguments can be either *constants* or *variables*. Constants such as

john
a
northern_dancer
mary

are all known as *atoms*. Integer values, which are dealt with in chapter 3, are also constants, but they are not defined as atoms. Remember, the general syntax rule about atoms is that they begin with a lower case letter and represent instantiated values. However there are exceptions to this rule which will be discussed later.

A useful feature of Prolog which we will find to be valuable to us in the construction of sophisticated programs is the ability to 'transform' phrases into a format which enables Prolog to treat them as atoms. This is achieved by enclosing the phrase or expression in single quotes, for example 'the Prolog programmer'. This feature is exploited fully in chapter 5.

Variables begin with a capital letter in general but, should you need to do so, the underline character (*not* the hyphen) may be used to classify a variable. For example

_x
_man

A third type of argument exists which we will refer to as a structure. Some structures, known as lists, are so important and powerful that we have devoted a separate section to their discussion. Here we are going to introduce the idea of using structures as arguments.

Suppose we wish to build a personnel recording system, a very common commercial application. Within that system we could have a factual assertion of the kind

employee (jones, ss2).

which we would take to mean "There is an employee named jones whose grade is stores superintendent, level 2". By employing a structural form of argument we can widen the scope of our system and make it more sympathetic to human dialogue, as shown below

employee (surname (jones), initial (h), grade (manager), level (1)).
employee (surname (jones), initial (p), grade (clerk), level (5)).
employee (surname (jones), initial (c), grade (stores_super), level (5)).

To access the information contained in this type of statement we use variables as before. There are two basic methods

(i) either we can address the whole structure by a variable as in

employee (W, X, Y, Z).

(ii) or we can address the arguments of the structures which themselves serve as arguments to the employee predicate, for example

employee (surname (W), initial (X), grade (Y), level (Z)).

By using the employee record

employee (surname (smith), initial (j), grade (programmer), level (7)).

we can illustrate the previous point. First set the goal.

?- employee (W, X, Y, Z).

Here we see that the variables are instantiated to full clauses and the solution returned will be

W = surname (smith)
X = initial (j)
Y = grade (programmer)
Z = level (7)

If we now specify the goal as

?- employee (surname (W), initial (X), grade (Y), level (Z)).

then the variables will be instantiated to the arguments of the four structures which themselves serve as arguments to the employee predicate. The answers returned using this form of questioning will be

W = smith
X = j
Y = programmer
Z = 7

If we wished to make the results particularly intelligible or the program easier to read we could take advantage of the fact that anything beginning with a capital letter is a variable, and phrase our question as

?-
employee (surname (Surname), initial (Initial), grade (Grade), level (Level)).

and we would receive the solution

Surname = smith
Initial = j
Grade = programmer
Level = 7

2.4 Exercise 4

Using the idea of structures, program a small personnel registration system. You could take students on a course, employees of a firm or members of a club as the people to be registered by the system.

2.5 The 'blank' variable

We have already seen that a variable can begin with a capital letter or the underline character. Furthermore we have seen how the underline character offers us a simple and convenient way of writing constants which need more than one word to describe them. There is, however, a third use for this symbol, which is perhaps more important than either of the other two — that is when it is used to represent the blank variable.

The blank variable is used in the situation where one needs to recognise the existence of an argument, but does not wish to instantiate it to a constant value. Once more, an example is probably the best way to demonstrate the idea.

Suppose we have the rule

husband (X) :- married (X, _).

What we are saying is that **X** is a husband if **X** is married to *anyone*, whose identity we do not need to know. All we require to know is that there is such a person.

Let us place this example in the context of a knowledge base.

married (joe, elsie).
married (fred, doris).
married (darren, tracey).
child (joe. elsie, ern).
child ͺᴊᴀᵣᵣen, tracey, justin).
boy (ern).
boy (justin).
son (X) :- child (_, _, X), boy (X).
husband (X) :- married (X,_).
wife (X) :- married (_, X).

You will notice that the rules are all designed to focus attention on one particular attribute of a certain individual. A most important point to note is that the first sub-goal of **son (X)** is **child (_, _, X)** which, because of the way that the assertions about **child** are stated (for example, **child (joe, elsie, ern)**), requires three arguments. Similarly, the first (and only) sub-goals of **husband (x)** and **wife (X)** are **married (X,_)** and **married (_, X)** respectively, both of which require two arguments. Similarly, the first (and only) sub-goals of **husband (X)** and **wife (X)** are describing the parents or the argument describing the marriage partner; *they cannot be dispensed with*.
Neither

      son (X) :- child (X).

nor

      husband (X) :- married (X).

would work in this example. The blank variable must be supplied to 'fill the gap', as it were.

Let us simulate a question and answer session using the example program

Prolog	*User*
?–	**husband (X).**
X = joe	;
X = fred	;
X = darren	;
no	
?–	**son (ern).**
yes	
?–	**son (X).**
X = ern	
yes	
?–	**child (_, _, X).**
X = ern	;
X = darren	
yes	
?–	**married (_, elsie).**
yes	
?–	**married (_, X).**
X = elsie	;
X = doris	;
X = tracy	;
no	
?–	**married (_,_,_).**
yes	
?–	. . . (session ends)

If you study the above example carefully, it will give you a good idea of how the blank variable is used. There will be plenty of further opportunities to examine this piece of syntax.

2.6 Search and pattern matching

We have introduced the way in which Prolog generates solutions by proving the success of goals in numerous examples. In this section we will attempt to summarise the way in which the all important searching mechanism works.

As we already know, there are two fundamental question formats. The first is when we ask Prolog to confirm or deny an assertion, for example

> **?– married (jack, mavis).**

and the second is when we ask Prolog to produce a solution, for example

> **?– married (jack, X).**

The first format utilises constants and the blank variable only, the second variables or a mixture of constants and variables.

We also know by now that a question can be resolved by matching with factual assertions or by the resolution of rules accompanied, finally, by matching with facts. At the end of the process we must always have factual assertions which allow solutions to be generated. A knowledge base consisting of only rules and variables cannot provide answers. Furthermore, to review the useful knowledge already gained, we know that some questions will have more than one set of answers which can be elicited by the use of the ; prompt symbol.

Essentially, there are three principles that should be understood.

(i) Solutions are identified by 'pattern matching' and a pattern match can take place only if both predicate and argument(s) match completely. Here are a few examples of this idea.

married (X, Y) pattern matches completely with the assertion **married (joe, elsie)** because the predicate 'married' is the same and the correct number of valid arguments is present in both. Notice that the variables **X** and **Y** are instantiated (assigned) to the constants **joe** and **elsie** respectively, as part of the pattern matching process.

owner (angela, Y) pattern matches with the head of the rule

> **owner (X, Y) :– human (X), cat (Y).**

and, assuming we have pattern matches for **human (angela)** and **cat (Y)** we can generate a solution, which will assign the name of the cat to the variable **Y** in the question. The variable **X** in the rule head matches with the atomic constant **angela** in the question, the variable **Y** in the question is instantiated to **Y** in the rule head and subsequently to the cat's name, if one exists. **married (X)** does *not* pattern match with **married (joe, elsie)** because the number of arguments differs.

married (X, Y) does *not* pattern match with **couple (joe, elsie)** because, even though the idea of married and couple may be similar, the predicates mismatch.

(ii) As a general principle the knowledge base is searched from 'top to bottom' — in other words the order in which the programmer writes statements into a serial file. Consider the following example which illustrates the idea that the order in which clauses are written is highly significant.

> **mother (mary, jesus).**
> **mother (jean, iain).**

If we put the following question

> **?– mother (X, Y).**

Then the first solution returned will be the one suggested by the first assertion in the knowledge base, that is

> **X = mary**
> **Y = jesus**

The other solution is obtained by the ; prompt, in other words the search will continue 'downwards'.

(iii) Rules are resolved from left to right; thus the head is examined first and the sub-goals in the body of the rule are examined from left to right.
Let us look at a simple example

> **clerk (jones).**
> **clerk (smith).**
> **typist (brown).**
> **manager (patel).**
> **manager (lee).**
> **supervises (X, Y) :– manager (X), clerk (Y).**
> **supervises (X, Y) :– clerk (X), typist (Y).**
> **supervises (X, Y) :– manager (X), typist (Y).**

Now we will analyse how some questions are resolved

(a) ?- clerk (jones).
Prolog goes to the 'top' of the knowledge base and pattern matches **clerk**. In
this question the argument is instantiated to **jones** and a full match can now take
place with the very first statement with the predicate **clerk** in the knowledge base.
The answer **yes** is returned and the question prompt reappears.

(b) ?- clerk (X).
Again the first statement is examined. Once more a pattern match can take place
on **clerk**. Since the question format contained the variable **X**, this can now be
instantiated to **jones** and the answer **X** = **jones** is returned. However, Prolog has
'marked the place' where a solution was found. If the prompt ; is now entered
the solution already given is ignored because Prolog continues to look for solutions
below the marker in the knowledge base. The solution **X** = **smith** is therefore
the next solution found.

(c) ?- supervises (jones, Y) or "who does jones supervise"?
Here, Prolog will go to the 'top' of the knowledge base and search for the first
clause that matches. There is no assertion that matches with **supervises**, but there
is a rule head which has the predicate **supervises** and two arguments and therefore a match is possible. The first rule to be examined is therefore

> supervises (X, Y) :- manager (X), clerk (Y).

and Prolog will attempt to use that rule. Notice that **X** is instantiated to **jones**
in the question, and the sub-goals are to be examined from left to right. For the
above rule to succeed it is necessary to obtain a match on

> manager (jones).

As you can see, that is not possible and therefore the attempt to satisfy the rule
fails, without the second sub-goal **clerk** being examined. The first rule gives no
solution and so Prolog moves 'down' the knowledge base to attempt to try and
find another matching assertion or rule, and encounters the rule

> supervises (X, Y) :- clerk (X), typist (Y).

The variable **X** remains instantiated to **jones** (we are still asking the same
question), and the sub-goals are examined from left to right. For the rule to
succeed, it is necessary to pattern match on an assertion or rule head of the form

> clerk (jones).

and Prolog succeeds using the first assertion in the knowledge base. The second sub-goal is then examined, and as you can see a match is possible on the third assertion

    typist (brown).

The variable **Y** is therefore instantiated to the constant **brown** and the correct solution **Y = brown** is obtained.

(d) ?- **supervises (X, Y).** or "who supervises who"?
This is a slightly more complex example, so we will number the steps which are taken to generate solutions.
(1) The predicate is **supervises** and the first clause to match with the correct predicate and the correct number of arguments is the rule

    supervises (X, Y) :- manager (X), clerk (Y).

The first sub-goal

    manager (X).

then needs to be evaluated in order to establish the truth or otherwise of the goal.
(2) Prolog now attempts to find the first clause that matches with **manager (X).** The match is possible on the fourth assertion and on making the match the variable **X** is instantiated to **patel**.
(3) The second sub-goal, **clerk (Y)**, now needs to succeed. Prolog now attempts to find the first clause to match the predicate **clerk**. The first statement matches and allows **Y** to be instantiated to **jones**.
(4) The first possible pair of answers is now returned, that is

    X = patel
    Y = jones

At this point the user can terminate the question. However, as you can see by inspection there are other solutions that could be returned. The next pair of names may be obtained by typing in a semi-colon.
(5) Prolog is now asked to find other solutions to the question. Prolog has remembered the first solution and has marked the database, and **X** has remained instantiated to **patel**. Further solutions for the sub-goal **clerk (Y)** will now be searched for, starting with the first clause in the knowledge base after **clerk (jones)**. As it happens, a further match succeeds with the assertion **clerk (smith)** and **Y** will therefore be instantiated to **smith**. However it is interesting to consider what happens when there are no other matches on **clerk**. Prolog will now *backtrack* in an attempt to try and find another solution for the sub-goal **manager (X)**, starting from the clauses below **manager (patel)** in the knowledge

base. As you can see, it will find the solution **X = lee**. The knowledge base is then searched from the *top* again in order to satisfy the sub-goal, **clerk (Y)**. We are searching from the top again because we are attempting to find all the clerks who are supervised by the **manager (X)**. The process of attempting to rematch a clause if the one immediately on its right fails is known as *backtracking*.

(6) If further solutions were requested, they would be generated in the order

X	Y
lee	jones
lee	smith
jones	brown
smith	brown
patel	brown
lee	brown

By now, we can see why the solutions would be given in that order; *it is because of the order of the assertions and rules in the knowledge base*. For simple programs like this example the order is usually unimportant; however, in advanced applications of Prolog, the order in which rules and assertions with the same number of predicates and arguments are written can be of crucial importance. It is therefore essential to understand how the search and pattern matching mechanism operates in the generation of solutions.

2.7 Exercise 5

Describe the processes whereby Prolog would resolve the goal **president (X, Y)**, from the knowledge base below:

```
member (jones, wentworth).
member (smith, wentworth).
member (brown, sunningdale).
member (thomson, wentworth).
candidate (smith, wentworth).
candidate (thomson, wentworth).
elected (smith).
elected (brown).
president (X, Y)  :- member (X, Y),
                     candidate (X, Y),
                     elected (X).
```

2.8 Diagrammatic representation of backtracking

It is interesting to note that the search mechanism of Prolog is a type of search known as a depth first search. If we analyse how the solutions to the question

supervises (X, Y) (section 2.6) are elicited, we find that we are searching a tree of the form shown below.

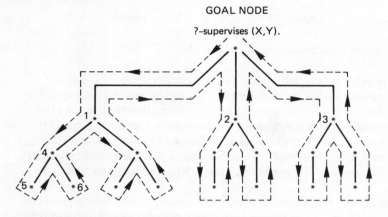

Node 1 = **supervises (X,Y):—manager (X), clerk (Y).**

Node 2 = **supervises (X,Y):— clerk (X), typist (Y).**

Node 3 = **supervises (X,Y):—manager (X), typist (Y)|.**

Node 4 = **manager (patel).**

Node 5 = **clerk (jones).**

Node 6 = **clerk (smith).**

A node is shown by the * symbol. A branch of the tree structure shown above is indicated by the lines joining the nodes. Each node represents a goal or sub-goal, as indicated above. The search always begins with the left-most branch which is attached to the node whose goal appears first in the knowledge base. You can see this from nodes 1, 2 and 3. The rules assigned to each of these appear in the same order as they do in the knowledge base. The dotted line shows how the solutions are obtained in traversing the tree. The graphic representation shows how the backtracking mechanism works. You can see that after the first solution is obtained (**X = patel, Y = jones**) at node 5, Prolog returns to node 4 in an attempt to resatisfy **clerk (Y)** which it may do by going to node 6. After this solution no more can be found, since there are no more assertions of the form **clerk (Y)** which implies no more branches from node 4. The backtracking mechanism therefore returns to node 1 and continues its search from there as shown.

2.9 Solutions to exercises

If you have understood the first two chapters, you will have realised that Prolog is flexible in the way it allows problems to be solved by programming. Therefore the solutions to exercises 4 and 5 are suggested solutions only, you may well have found a different and better approach.

Exercise 4

This example registers members of a golf club:

> member (name (ash), initial (a), subscription (full), h_cap (12).
> member (name (brown), initial (b), subscription (half), h_cap (20)).
> member (name (cooper), initial (h), subscription (full, h_cap (18)).
> member (name (day), initial (p), subscription (junior), h_cap (9)).
> weekday_member (X) :- member (name (X),_, subscription (half),_).
> weekday_member (X) :- member (name (X),_, subscription (junior),_).
> full_member (X) :- member (name (X),_ , subscription (full),_).

As you can see, the system registers name, initial, class of subscription and handicap. There are also some simple rules which define the status of the members — those who may play only from Monday to Friday and those who may play on any day of the week. The rules utilise the blank variable because the classification does not require the initial or handicap of the member to be considered, only the name and type of subscription are necessary. You may care to code this example and see for yourself how it works, and then expand it to take account of good players and other relevant factors.

Exercise 5

The following steps are taken to generate a solution.

(1) For the goal **president (X, Y)** to succeed, a match is made on the rule head **president (X, Y).** and then the sub-goals **member (X, Y), candidate (X, Y)**, and **elected (X)** must succeed from left to right in the usual manner. First the sub-goal **member (X, Y)** allows **X** to become instantiated to **jones** and **Y** to **wentworth**. However that requires the goal **candiate (jones, wentworth)** to succeed, which is not possible.
(2) Prolog now tries to re-establish **member (X, Y)** using the built in backtracking mechanism and succeeds with **X** instantiated to **smith** and **Y** instantiated to **wentworth**. The sub-goal **candidate (smith, wentworth)** is then attempted and succeeds. The final sub-goal **elected (smith)** succeeds and the answers

> **X = smith**
> **Y = wentworth**

are returned. Note that brown is not a president of sunningdale because he is not a candidate.

3 Arithmetic, the "Cut" Symbol, and Recursion

In this chapter we shall discuss three important features of the Prolog language, none of which merits a whole chapter to itself. Although we have included these in the same chapter, we would not wish to give the reader the impression that these language features are in any way dependent on one another — it is simply convenient to introduce them all at the same stage of learning, and as we shall see the three features may be combined into complex program statements.

3.1 Arithmetic

It should be made clear from the outset that Prolog was not a language designed for mathematical applications, and there are other languages (such as APL, Q'NIAL and ALGOL) which are far better for specialist applications. However more recent implementations of Prolog do offer standard facilities for manipulating real numbers (see appendixes 1 and 2). Edinburgh DEC-10 Prolog supports only integer arithmetic, and the reader should bear that in mind when considering the following material. Furthermore, the other versions of Prolog on which this book is based (see the Preface) have special function sets for integer arithmetic but the operations described in the following sections are applied to real numbers. We recommend that readers familiarise themselves with the arithmetic facilities on their particular version of Prolog. The examples that follow are based on the DEC-10 integer functions, but can easily be applied to other Prolog systems.

3.1.1 The is operator

This operator is necessary for the use of arithmetic beyond the most simple level. In many ways it can be seen to take the place of the = sign in standard arithmetic. This is necessary because in Prolog the = sign is used for making a logical check, not for assigning a value. Thus the goals

    man = man
    3 = 3

will always succeed whereas

31

man = woman
3 = 4

will always fail.

The expression

A is B − 1

has the effect of instantiating the value of variable **A** to one less than that of **B**. Similarly, the statement

A is B∗C.

instantiates **A** to the product of **B** and **C** and is equivalent to the algebraic statement

let A = B × C

You will see more examples of the **is** operator later in the chapter.

3.1.2 Standard arithmetical operators

These are the same operators that are to be found in most computer languages

+ addition
− subtraction
∗ multiplication
/ division

Examples of the use of each are given below.

Addition
The **+** operator carries out integer addition. Thus the expression

X is 3 + 6

has the effect of instantiating **X** to the value of **9**. Similarly the expression

X is Y + Z.

causes **X** to be instantiated to the sum of **Y** and **Z** (assuming that **Y** and **Z** are instantiated to integer values or expressions). Finally, the expression

X is Y + Z + 2

has the effect of instantiating **X** to the sum of **Y**, **Z** and **2** (assuming that **Y** and **Z** are instantiated to integer values or expressions).

Subtraction
If you have understood how the addition operator works then you will have no difficulty in understanding how the subtraction operator functions. The expression

X is 5 − 3

causes **X** to be instantiated to **2**. The expression

X is Y + Z − 5.

results in **X** being instantiated to the sum of **Y** and **Z** less **5** (assuming that **Y** and **Z** are instantiated to integer values or expressions).

Multiplication
The ∗ operator causes multiplication to be carried out. Thus

X is 2∗3.

results in **X** being instantiated to **6**. The expression

X is Y ∗ 3.

results in **X** being instantiated to three times the value of **Y**.

Division
The / operator is used to carry out *integer* division. Thus the expressions

X is 15/5 and X is 16/5

will both result in **X** being instantiated to **3**. However, you will notice that in the second expression the division is not exact, there is a remainder of one. In order to access the remainder of an inexact division the **mod** operator is used. Thus the pair of expressions

X is 16/5, Y is 16 mod 5.

will result in **X** being instantiated to **3** and **Y** to the remainder, **1**.

Using more than one operator
We have already seen an example of addition and subtraction being used in the

same expression, but all the operators can be used together quite easily. Sometimes brackets are necessary to make the sense of the expression clear, although in general * and / take precedence over + and −. Thus the expression

X is 2*3 − 4.

will be evaluated by first multiplying 2 and 3 together and then subtracting 4 from the product (the other obvious possibility would be to multiply 2 by the difference of 3 and 4).

It is recommended that you get into the habit of using brackets for compound expressions of this kind, if only because you can follow your own coding with complete clarity. For example, the proposition that the value of **X** is the product of **A** and **B** divided by **C** and added to **D** is best written as

X is ((A*B) /C) + D.

3.1.3 Comparing integers and integer expressions

Equality
The system operator =:= is used to test equality. For example, the goal

X + Y − Z =:= 3.

will succeed providing that the instantiated values of **X, Y** and **Z** cause the expression to evaluate to 3 (for example, **X** = 1, **Y** = 4, **Z** = 2).

Inequality
The operator =/= succeeds if integer expressions are not equal, thus the goal

X =/= 3 + 5.

will succeed providing that **X** does not have the value **B**.

Comparative size of expressions
If we wish to test whether an integer or integer expression is greater than another, then we may use the familiar mathematical symbol for 'greatter than", >. Thus the goal

6 > X.

will succeed providing that **X** takes an instantiated value of **5** or less. Furthermore, the symbol >= represents "greater than or equal to". Thus the goals

7 > = 6. and 7 > = 7.

will both succeed.

Similarly, there are provisions made for the tests "less than" and 'less than or equal to", the respective symbols being < and =<.

3.2 Exercise 6

(i) Write a Prolog program to output the result of dividing one integer by another in the form X remainder Y.
(ii) Write a Prolog program to calculate the average value of two numbers.

3.3 The "cut" symbol

This is represented in Prolog by the exclamation mark ! and is in fact like a predicate that is built into the language. It is unlike other predicates you have encountered in that it is represented by a symbol rather than a word or or expression and that it has no arguments. The effect of the cut is to restrict the working of the search mechanism in Prolog and its action is somewhat like passing through a one-way street in a car; you go through it one way to achieve a goal but you cannot return in the reverse direction.

As you will have seen from reading chapter 2, Prolog attempts to prove the success of goals (generate solutions) in a particular manner which frequently involves, particularly when sub-goals need to be satisfied, the backtracking process. When the cut is included as part of a goal definition it inhibits the 'route' that Prolog takes to satisfy a goal because although it is possible to pass the cut to try to satisfy a goal, it is not possible to pass it on backtracking, hence the one-way street analogy.

Let us look at a simple example of the cut in use. Consider the following knowledge base

```
parent (john).
parent (fred).
parent (jean).
male (john).
male (fred).
female (jean).
father (X) :- parent (X), male (X), !.
```

If you look at the rule defining **father** you will see that the cut symbol appears as a sub-goal. Were the cut not present and we asked the question

```
?- father (X).
```

the solutions **X = john** and **X = fred** would be returned; the second in response to a semi-colon prompt.

However with the cut included in the definition of **father** only one answer will be generated, **X = john,** and the ; prompt will elicit the response **no.** This is because, first Prolog will evaluate the sub-goals **parent** and **male** — instantiating **X** to **john** in both cases — and thereafter it cannot pass backwards past the cut to resatisfy for another value (which would normally result in **X** being instantiated to **fred)** and therefore cannot generate a second solution.

3.3.1 Tree structure with "cut"

As we have seen, the cut is used to prevent backtracking. It may therefore be thought of as pruning the search tree that would normally be generated as a result of backtracking. Suppose we return to the knowledge base given in section 2.6 and add the rule

> **find _a_supervisor (X, Y) :- supervises (X, Y), !.**

which is saying "find one supervisor X who supervises Y". If we now ask the question

> **?- find_a_supervisor (X, Y).**

then the search tree will be as shown. Notice how the cut prevents the search returning to node 3 and hence effectively prunes the tree that would be produced were the cut not present (the pruned portion is shown by broken lines).

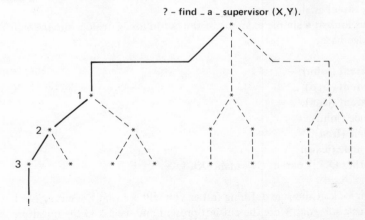

At this stage we have introduced the cut symbol and applied it to a simple example in order to demonstrate the concept of using the cut to restrict backtracking. In fact the value of the cut becomes more apparent when applied to complex program structures and in later chapters there will be more examples of the cut in use.

3.4 Exercise 7

```
parent (john).
parent (fred).
parent (jean).
male (john).
male (fred).
female (jean).
father (X) :- parent (X), male (X), !.
mother (X) :- parent (X), !, female (X).
```

Using the above knowledge base, what effect will the inclusion of the cut symbol have on the way in which the questions

?- father (X). and **?- mother (X).**

are answered?

3.5 Recursion in Prolog

One of the more powerful techniques in programming is that of recursion, wherein we define a procedure that can 'go back into itself' until a programming task is completed. For those of you not familiar with advanced programming terminology the technique of iteration utilises the 'if, then, else' structure for directing program logic whereas when a rule or process features a re-statement of that rule or process as part of its definition it is said to be recursive — a lighthearted version of this appears in the spoof definition "recursion — (see recursion)".

The structure and syntax of Prolog, as we shall see, lend themselves particularly well to the elegant and concise statement of recursive procedures and rules. Once mastered, the technique of programming recursively extends the problem solving power of the language.

3.5.1 Defining a procedure in terms of itself

As we have already said, the essence of generating a successful recursion in Prolog is the ability to define a predicate in terms of itself. However, certain limitations, all of which are quite logical, have to be kept in mind. Let us start with a simple example of a recursive definition: the problem of defining the ancestry of a human or animal. Since the question of descent is so important to breeders of thoroughbred racehorses, we will choose that as our example.

Taking the 1984 Derby winner, Secreto, as our subject we have the following blood line

Secreto sired by Northern Dancer sired by Neartic sired by Nearco
sired by Nasrullah.

In order to use a Prolog program to give the ancestry of Secreto we might
proceed in the most obvious (that is, non-recursive) manner and program as
follows

```
sire (secreto, northern_dancer).
grandsire (secreto, neartic).
great_grandsire (secreto, nearco).
great_great_grandsire (secreto, nasrullah).
ancestor (X, Y) :- sire (X, Y).
ancestor (X, Y) :- grandsire (X, Y).
ancestor (X, Y) :- great_grandsire (X, Y).
ancestor (X, Y) :- great_great_grandsire (X, Y).
```

and when we ask the question

```
?- ancestor (secreto, Y).
```

we obtain the correct solutions, northern_dancer, neartic, nearco and
nasrullah.

Now, although this method does work (incidentally you may be able to
think of several similar ways of obtaining the same solution), it does have
several disadvantages, as follows.

(1) It is a rather cumbersome method which you can clearly see would involve
    the programming of vast numbers of similar assertions and rules if the
    system were to accommodate a substantial number of horses.
(2) If we wished to extend it to take in another generation, an assertion
    of the rather tedious great_great_great_grandfather format would be
    needed, as would another rule establishing the relation as an ancestor.
(3) If we introduce Secreto's half brother, Nijinsky, to the system we would
    have to reprogram the system despite the fact that all male ancestors belong
    to both Secreto and Nijinsky.

It would clearly be much better if we could accomplish the whole thing by
simply asserting the relationship sire and using our knowledge to define an
ancestor of the sire as also being an ancestor of the son. We can do precisely
that by using recursion as follows

```
sire (secreto, northern_dancer).
sire (nijinsky, northern_dancer).
sire (northern_dancer, neartic).
```

sire (neartic, nearco).
sire (nearco, nasrullah).
ancestor (X, Y) :-sire (X, Y).
ancestor (X, Y) :-sire (X, Z), ancestor (Z, Y).

The first rule in the knowledge base establishes the essential relationship that
a sire is an ancestor. "If the sire of X is Y then Y is the ancestor of X". The
second rule introduces recursion whereby the ancestor of the sire is also the
ancestor of the son. "If the sire of X is Z and the ancestor of Z is Y then Y
is the ancestor of X". Work out the above rules and satisfy yourself that they
are logically consistent.

You can, we hope, see that it is a much more convenient and flexible format
than the first example and note that it allows us to introduce Nijinsky to the knowledge base by programming the additional assertion

sire (nijinsky, northern_dancer).

To demonstrate how the example program would work, here is a dialogue
between the system and the user.

Prolog	*User*
?-	**ancestor (secreto, Y).**
Y = northern_dancer	**;**
Y = neartic	**;**
Y = nearco	**;**
Y = nasrullah	**;**
no	
?-	**ancestor (nijinsky, Y).**
Y = northern_dancer	**. . . (session ends)**

3.5.2 How does it work?

Using the same example, this is what happens when the user asks the program
about the ancestors of secreto.

(1) The first time through, **X** is instantiated by the question to **secreto,** and a
match is made on the first rule in the knowledge base. There is an assertion
sire(secreto, northern_dancer) in the knowledge base and therefore **Y** can be
instantiated to **northern_dancer** without the second rule being used.
(2) When the semi-colon is typed to seek another solution, the first rule alone
cannot provide the solution because there is only one assertion that gives
information about the sire of secreto in the knowledge base, and that soluion
has already been given. Therefore, the second rule is used, with **X** instantiated
to **secreto** as before. The assertion **sire (secreto, northern_dancer)** causes **Z** to

be instantiated to **northern_dancer** in the body of the second rule. The second
sub-goal in the body of the second rule therefore becomes

   ancestor (northern_dancer, Y).

   To evaluate this sub-goal Prolog goes back to the first rule, which in turn
causes the goal

   sire (northern_dancer, Y).

to be attempted. This sub-goal can match with the assertion

   sire (northern_dancer, neartic).

which causes **Y** to become instantiated to **neartic**. The solution is therefore
generated (**Y = neartic**). The other solutions (**Y = nearco**) and (**Y = nasrullah**)
are generated in the same manner.

3.5.3 Recursion in arithmetic

It can be particularly useful to program recursive routines for arithmetic. As a
simple example take the case of calculating the value of a factorial of a number.
(If you are unfamiliar with the definition of the factorial of a number, it is the
product of the number multiplied by all the numbers below it, and applies
to positive integers only. Thus, the factorial of 5 is 120, that is

   $5 \times 4 \times 3 \times 2 \times 1 = 120$

By definition the factorial of zero is 1.)
Here is the routine to perform the calculation

```
fac (∅, 1).
fac (X, Xf) :- Y is X-1,
              fac (Y, Yf),
              Xf is Yf * X.
```

The routine relies on the fact that the factorial of any number can be derived
by multiplying that number by the factorial of the number immediately below
it. Reverting to the first example for clarity — the factorial of five is derived by
multiplying 5 by the factorial of 4.
   The first statement, **fac (∅, 1)**, is known as the 'boundary condition' and
it is necessary for two reasons. Firstly to allow the factorial of ∅ to be calculated, but secondly, and more importantly, to prevent the routine recursing
into negative numbers and continuing indefinitely.

The main part of the rule could be stated as follows

"The factorial Xf of an integer X is calculated as follows: let Y = X − 1 and let Yf be the factorial of Y. The factorial of Xf is then the product of X and Yf''.

As you can see, the routine will proceed recursively by reducing the value of the number to be operated on until the boundary condition $\emptyset$ is reached. The factorial of $\emptyset$ is given in the first assertion which then allows the factorial value required to be calculated. As you can see, the definition of **fac** actually allows for a multiple solution to be generated for the factorial of $\emptyset$ (that is, by using both the **fac** clauses). To make the routine more elegant we could introduce the cut in order to tell Prolog not to use any other assertions or rules of the form **fac($\emptyset$, 1)** once it has used our boundary condition assertion. The modified definition now becomes

    fac ($\emptyset$, 1) :-!.
    fac (X, Xf) :- Y is X−1,
                fac (Y, Yf),
                Xf is Yf ∗ X.

Chapter 4 and subsequent chapters contain other examples of recursion.

3.6 Exercise 8

(i) Given the following knowledge base, add the necessary rules in order to allow ancestors to be defined, using a recursive definition.

    parents (jim, john, ellen).
    parents (john, bill, doris).
    parents (ellen, jack, mavis).
    parents (bill, joe, flossie).
    parents (doris, bert, mabel).
    parents (jack, crispin, samantha).
    parents (mavis, jock, alison).

All the above assertions are of the form **parents (X, Y, Z)** and read "the parents of X are Y and Z".

(ii) The mathematical expression N c R is derived as follows; divide the factorial of N by the product of the factorial of R and the factorial of (N−R). Program a procedure to calculate N c R.

(iii) Write a program to calculate the value of an integer X to the power of an integer N.

3.7 Solutions to exercises

Exercise 6

(i) There are two ways of approaching this, depending on whether the arithmetic is carried out on an integer basis (DEC-10) or a real number basis (Quintus Prolog, Prolog 1).
For integer based arithmetic:
Use A and B to represent the integers (A to be divided by B); X is to be the quotient and Y the remainder

> **division (A, B, X, Y) :- X is A/B,**
> **Y is A mod B.**

If you were to question the system about, for example, the division of 17 by 5, it would be a good idea to put the question like this

> **division (17, 5, Quotient, Remainder).**

which would generate the solution

> **Quotient = 3**
> **Remainder = 2**

For real number based arithmetic

> **division (A, B, X, Y) :- X is A//B,**
> **Y is A mod B.**

Note the // symbol which is used to declare integer division.

(ii)

> **average (X, Y, A) :- A is (X + Y)/2**

(Note that the integer based system — that is, DEC-10 — will produce a different result in some cases than will the real number based systems. For example

> **?- average (3, 4, A).**

will produce **A = 3** (DEC-10)
or **A = 3.5** (Quintus, Prolog-1)

Exercise 7

In the definition of the rule for **father**, the position of the cut symbol will allow one solution to be generated, **X = john**. After that, no further solutions can be generated by backtracking and a semi-colon prompt (which without the cut would result in **X = fred** being generated) will elicit the answer **no**.

The cut in the rule defining **mother** prevents any solutions being generated. This is because Prolog first attempts to prove the sub-goal **parent**, and instantiates **X** to **john**. The cut then succeeds and the third sub-goal **female (X)** then fails because **X** is instantiated to **john**. However, because of the cut no attempt can be made to backtrack to **parent (X)** and hence the goal **mother (X)** fails.

Exercise 8

(i) In this example it is necessary to define an ancestor as a parent or the ancestor of a parent. However, no predicate for parent exists (although there is one for parents), therefore we must first define

    parent (X, Y) :- parents (X, Y, _).
    parent (X, Y) : - parents (X, _, Y).

Now for the recursive rule to define ancestor

    ancestor (X, Y) :- parent (X, Y).
    ancestor (X, Y) :- parent (X, Z), ancestor (Z, Y).

(ii) First, define the rule for factorial as before

    factorial (∅, 1) :- !.
    factorial (N, Nf) : - R is N − 1,
                   factorial (R, Rf),
                   Nf is N∗Rf.

Now we can use the above definition to build the more complex rules

    combine (N, R, C) :- factorial (N, Nf),
                      factorial (R, Rf),
                      X is N − R,
                      factorial (X, Xf),
                      C is Nf/ (Xf∗Rf).

(iii)

```
exp (X, Ø, 1) :- !.
exp (X, N, E) :- R is N - 1,
            exp (X, R, Er),
            E is Er*X.
```

4 Lists and Complex Structures

4.1 Lists in Prolog

Lists are an important tool in modern mathematics and symbolic computing. Those of you who are familiar with them will know that lists are an essential structure in the LISP language. Our objective here is to show how lists can be used to enhance the power and scope of Prolog programs.

First then, what is a list? In simple terms it is a sequence of single elements that may (and in practical programming, often do) bear some relation to each other. Here are some examples of lists

(i) **a, b, c, d, e**
(ii) **lion, tiger, puma, lynx**
(iii) **f, r, 3, X, y, z**

As you can see, (i) and (ii) are lists which contain members of a particular category — letters of the alphabet and big cats respectively. The third example is a collection of constants, integers and variables. Any syntactically correct Prolog element (constant, variable or structure) may appear in a Prolog list; this includes the case where one list is part of another as we shall see.

4.2 The structure of lists

The value of lists in a Prolog program is reduced if we cannot address the individual elements that go to make up the list. For that reason, it is necessary to use the concept of splitting the list into two parts, the *head* and the *tail*. The *head* of the list is the first element of the list. The *tail* of the list is the remainder of the list whatever it may contain.

This is how the idea works. The list **lion, tiger, lynx, puma** is split into head and tail as follows

head = **lion**
tail = **tiger, lynx, puma**

It is worth stating that *the tail of the list is itself a list*; this is important.

The list

sid, doris

is split as follows

head = **sid**
tail = **doris**

Following on from the previous example, where it was stated that the tail of
a list is itself a list, you might ask whether it is also the case when the tail has
only a single element. The answer is yes, a single element can still be seen as
a list.

The next obvious question, then, is whether it is possible to split a single
element list into a head and a tail. Again the answer is yes, but in order to do
so we need to introduce another important idea, the *empty list*. If it was necessary to split a single element list (for example, **john**), into a head and a tail,
it could be done as follows

head = **john**
tail = **the empty list**

Logically the empty list is somewhat akin to the more familiar concepts of
zero, the empty set and the void. It is a useful and necessary concept in the use
of lists within Prolog programs. From the previous examples you can deduce
that a list with no elements presents us with no logical problems and we can
just designate it as the empty list.

4.3 Special list notation

In order to make practical use of the ability to split lists into head and tail,
Prolog provides a special notation with which to define lists in programs. There
are two special symbols which are used.

(1) The square open/close brackets
These are used to denote the beginning and end of a list respectively. For
example

[a, b, c, d]
[lion, tiger, lynx, puma]
[X]

The empty list is represented as [] .

(2) The separator symbol

This is written as ¦ and is used to allow a list to be represented as a head and a tail. The element to the left of the separator is taken as the head of the list, that to the right as the tail of the list. Thus to represent a list as two variables, the head and the tail, it is possible to write it as

[H¦T]

using the separator symbol to define the split representation.

4.4 Using lists and list notation

The best way to show how lists and their contents may be accessed in a Prolog program is to simulate an example terminal session. Here we will assume that our knowledge base consists only of a single clause with the predicate **letters** taking, as the single argument, the list [a, b, c, d].

The assertion would be represented as follows

letters ([a, b, c, d]).

Now we will perform some simple operations on the list.

Prolog	*User*
?–	letters (X).
X = [a, b, c, d]	
?–	letters ([H¦T]).
H = a	
T = [b, c, d]	
?–	letters ([X, Y¦T]).
X = a	
Y = b	
T = [c, d]	
?–	letters ([H¦_]).
H = a	
?–	letters ([_, [H¦T]]).
H = b	
T = [c, d]	... (session ends)

4.5 Exercise 9

A knowledge base contains these clauses

fish ([shark, pike, salmon, cod]).
birds ([hawk, dove, sparrow, canary]).

and the following questions are asked by the user

    (i) **fish ([H¦T])**.
   (ii) **birds ([_¦T])**.
  (iii) **birds ([H1, H2¦T])**.
  (iv) **birds (Birds)**.
   (v) **fish ([shark, X, salmon, Y]**.
  (vi) **birds (X, Y, Z)**.

What answers will the system return?

4.6 *Incorporating more complex data structures in lists*

Those of you familiar with LISP will have noticed that the head–tail notation is very closely allied to the LISP intrinsics CAR and CDR. (Do not worry if you do not know LISP, the point is incidental.) It is important that you understand how to access and manipulate the contents of lists and you should be sure that you can complete and understand exercise 9 before you proceed with this section.

Up to now we have used as examples lists which have *atoms* as their members. However, it is equally possible to construct lists which have more complex structures as members. For example

    employee_record (smith, [john, [sales, manager], london, [january, 1982]]).
    employee_record (brown, [jim, [prod, manager], luton, [june, 1983]]).

Thus the predicate **employee_record** (used here to hold a small personnel database) takes two arguments, the first the name of the employee, the second the list containing details about the employee. Here is an example terminal session to illustrate how the information contained in the list could be accessed.

Prolog	*User*
?–	**employee_record (Name, Details)**.
Name = smith	
Details = [john, [sales, manager],	
london, [january, 1982]]	
?–	**employee_record (brown, [_, Title,**
	Base,_]).
Title = [prod, manager]	
Base = luton	**. . . (session ends)**

Note that the format of the first question assigns the value of the complete details list to the second argument. However, the second question demonstrates the flexibility of the list structure for storing data, in that although the list represents only one argument to the **employee_record** predicate, the structure of that argument can itself be analysed by Prolog as shown in the example. This is an invaluable technique that can be used to great effect in the writing of complex programs.

4.7 Manipulating the contents of lists

The basis for success with these techniques is an understanding of the structure of lists (that is, the head – tail concept), and the application of recursion.

First, consider the question of whether or not a single element is an entry in a given list. To begin with we know that an element which represents the head of a list must be an entry in that list and we can use that property to write a boundary condition as follows

> **entry (E, L) :– L = [E¦_] .**

which states that "E is an entry in a list L, if L is made up of a head E and any tail" (hence the blank variable).

Now that you have thoroughly understood the list structure and the way in which Prolog works, you can probably see a more elegant way of writing the first clause of the procedure, that is

> **entry (E, [E¦_]).**

From now on we shall adopt this more compact format for these types of clauses.

So far we have dealt with the simple case where the head of a list is an entry in it. Now we need a second (recursive) clause which will allow all other entries to be identified. To construct that rule we use the property that any entry in the tail of a list must also be an entry in the list itself

> **entry (E, [_¦T]) :– entry (E, T).**

"E is an entry in a list if the list comprises any head and a tail T, which contains E".

Taking the pair of clauses defining the procedure

> **entry (E, [E¦_]).**
> **entry (E, [_¦T]) :– entry (E, T).**

we will trace the resolution of the question

> **?– entry (E, [a, b, c]).**

(i) The first solution is found by matching on the first clause, where the variable **E** is instantiated to the head of the list **[a, b, c]**, that is, **a**.

(ii) If we ask for another solution by entering the ; prompt it is clear that the first clause cannot directly provide it because **E** = **a** has already been returned. The search process therefore continues with the second clause wherein **T** is instantiated to **[b, c]**. It is important to understand that the recursive structure of the second clause now 'forces' a return to the first clause. However, after the second clause has been invoked the second argument to the first clause has changed. The list on which the first clause now has to operate has been changed from **[a, b, c]** to **[b, c]** and the head of the list now takes the value **b**, thereby allowing a second solution, **b**, to be generated. The third and last solution is generated in a similar manner to produce the answer **E** = **c**. Notice that the second clause can never directly provide a solution; its function is to remove successive heads from the front of the list before forcing a return to the first clause, which can then provide successive solutions.

4.7.1 Using *entry* to define other useful rules

We are now going to use the rules for entry to define the idea of membership of a particular category. Consider the small knowledge base

> employees (manager, [brown, jones, smith]).
> employeeds (clerical, [whyte, payne, clare]).
> employees (manual, [hempstead, burnham, hall]).

In order to establish an individual as, for example, a manager we can see that it is first necessary to establish the category **manager**, and second to search the list of managers. This is one method of achieving this

> manager (M) :– employees (manager, L),
>   entry (M, L).

(**entry** is defined as shown previously).

Furthermore, we can see that an employee is a wider category, that is, an employee is an entry in any one of the three lists we have specified. We can define an employee as follows

> employee (E) :– employees (_, L),
>   entry (E, L).

4.7.2 Joining two lists together

Suppose we want to join (or concatenate) two lists. For example we may wish to take the two lists $[a, b, c]$ and $[d, e, f]$ and join them to form the list $[a, b, c, d, e, f]$. Here is one method of achieving this

concatenate ([ ] , X, X).
concatenate ([H|X] , Y, [H|Z]) :– concatenate (X, Y, Z).

Thus the question

?– concatenate ([a, b, c] , [d, e, f] , L).

will elicit the response

L = [a, b, c, d, e, f]

The procedure works by recursively removing the head of the first list $[a, b, c]$. So the first time the procedure is called the element **a** is removed from the list, the second time **b** is removed and so on. This recursive calling continues because of the rule definition and is terminated when a match takes place with the first clause in the rule, that is **concatenate ([ ] , X, X)**. When this match takes place we have proved that the last head to be removed from the first list becomes the head of the result. As the recursive loop is exited the successive heads of the first list are added to the resultant list **L**.

4.7.3 Determining the nth term of a list

Here we wish to find out which element in a list is in the nth position. For example we may wish to access the third element. This can be done by removing N elements of a list recursively. The variable R keeps track of how many elements have been removed. When R = 1, then X is assigned to the Nth element.

nth (X, 1, [X|_]).
nth (X, N, [_|L]) :– R is N–1,
                     nth (X, R, L).

There are many more of these kinds of rules that can be applied to lists. Here are some for you to try.

4.8 Exercise 10

(i) Define the last entry in a list.
(ii) Remove an element of a list from that list leaving a new list (for example, **remove (a, [b, a, c] , L)** gives **L = [b, c]**.

4.9 Solutions to exercises

Exercise 9

(i) H = shark
   T = [pike, salmon, cod]
(ii) T = [dove, sparrow, canary]
(iii) H1 = hawk
   H2 = dove
   T = [sparrow, canary]
(iv) Birds = [hawk, dove, sparrow, canary]
(v) X = pike
   Y = cod
(vi) This is an incorrect question format.

Exercise 10

(i) last (X, [X]).
   last (X, [_¦L] :- last (X, L).
(ii) remove (X, [X¦T] , L) :- remove (X, T, L), !.
   remove (X, [X¦T] , T).
   remove (X, [H¦T], [H¦L]) :- remove (X, T, L).

Suggested project

Use the features of lists and the procedures for manipulating their contents
to set up and maintain a small database about something of interest to you.

5 *Interactive Programming using Prolog*

In this chapter we are going to examine some of the features of Prolog that allow you to write interactive programs. An interactive program is one that carries on a dialogue with the user and is capable of responding to requests input by the user. In some ways it is rather like carrying on a conversation with another person, and although most computer programs are somewhat more limited in their responses, one of the objectives of the Fifth Generation programme is to build computer systems that can respond to human users in much the same way as another human being would do.

Although Prolog can be used in a variety of ways, some of which require little or no interactive facilities, there is no doubt that most applications of the language are considerably enhanced by the provision of a 'user friendly' interface. The creation of such an interface depends essentially on the ability to do the following

  (i) The program should be able to accept input from the user.
 (ii) The program should be able to respond in a meaningful manner to that input.
(iii) The program should be able to output intelligible responses to the user.

Before proceeding with this chapter we would like to point out that we are going to make a considerable leap forward. Our intention in the first four chapters has been to provide you with the 'raw materials' with which you can construct Prolog programs. By the time you have assimilated the content of this chapter you should be able to write complete working programs and you should be ready to proceed to the more advanced uses of the language described in chapters 6, 7 and 8.

5.1 Input of information to the program

It is necessary at this stage to introduce you to some of the system predicates of the Prolog language. We have seen how it is possible for the programmer to define his or her own predicates. In addition to that facility, Prolog provides a range of system predicates which do not need to be defined by the programmer, but they can be used in the same way as a user-defined predicate. Several of these system predicates are of use to us in the development of interactive programs.

5.1.1 The **read** predicate

This predicate takes one argument, and causes a term to be read from the
user's terminal. Thus the goal **read (X)** always succeeds and has the effect of
causing the program to accept a term input from the user terminal. To take a
very simple example, suppose we wish to enter the word **password** to a Prolog
program. Here is a small program that will perform this function

```
get_pass: - read (X), test_pass (X).
test_pass (password) :- ok.
test_pass (_) :- error.
```

(Notice that we have introduced the concept of defining a predicate with no
arguments. This can be useful if we do not wish to know any information about
the values of the arguments in the body of the rule. It can also be a useful
technique to use predicates with no argument to invoke, or in some cases
simply label, a procedure or group of procedures.)
    Here is the terminal session that could follow (assume that we have defined
the predicates **ok** and **error** elsewhere in the knowledge base).

Prolog	*User*
?-	get_pass.
¦: (this is the prompt symbol)	password.

After the input of the word, Prolog would attempt to execute the **test_pass (X)**
goal. If the word were password the **ok** goal would be attempted, if anything
else were entered then Prolog would attempt to execute the error goal.
    You should have noticed from the above example that, on entering the word
password, X became instantiated to **password** and that value was passed over to
the second sub-goal of the **get_pass** goal, which tests to see that the correct
word has been input.
    In one simple example we have shown how it is possible to have the program
accept input from the user and then to respond to the input in a meaningful
way. There are other methods available to us to input information to a program
but first we will complete the interactive cycle by demonstrating how output
from the program to the user can be generated.

5.2 Output of information to the user

There are several ways in which this can be achieved, but we will start with
the most straightforward, the use of another system predicate.

5.2.1 The **write** predicate

This takes one term as its argument and causes that term to be written to the
user's terminal. Suppose that we wish to input the name of an animal from the
terminal and then to output the name of the natural enemy of that animal to
the terminal. The program might look something like this

```
enemy (frog, snake).
enemy (deer, wolf).
enemy (cat, dog).
find_enemy: - read (X), enemy (X, Y), write (Y).
```

Here is an example terminal session using the above knowledge base

Prolog	User
?–	find_enemy.
¦:	deer.
wolf	
?–	find_enemy.
¦:	frog.
snake	. . . (session ends)

The program operates as follows. First the user invokes the procedure by
typing in the predicate **find_enemy**. The first sub-goal is **read (X)** which is
used to tell the system which animal it has to find an enemy for. The prompt
symbol ¦: is then generated and the user replies with the response **deer**, which
instantiates **X** to **deer**. The second sub-goal is then attempted and matches with
the assertion **enemy (deer, wolf)**, so **Y** is instantiated to **wolf**. Finally the value
to which **Y** is instantiated is written to the terminal screen.

Obviously, we could achieve a similar result by entering questions in a more
rudimentary format, that is **enemy (deer, Y)**, and receive the response **Y = wolf**.
However we hope that you will agree that the solution using **read** and **write**
is more elegant and flexible, not least because it eliminates the rather cumbersome response format of **Y** = this, that and the other.

5.2.2 Holding text in the form of a list

This is useful if we wish to output phrases and sentences to the terminal; it is
possible to hold them as list elements and define a predicate to output the
list contents on to the screen. For example, let us define the predicate **screen**
to perform the above operation.

```
screen ([ ]): - !.
screen ([H¦T]) :- write (H), write (' '), screen (T).
```

All that we are saying is that we should output the elements in the list on to the screen, with three spaces between each character.

Here is how we could use it to improve the enemy program (remember from chapter 2 that we can utilise the single quote notation to represent phrases as atoms).

```
find_enemy:- screen (['Please enter the name of an animal.',
'I will then tell you the name of the natural enemy'],
        read (X),
        enemy (X, Y),
        write (Y).
```

Here is how the program would operate.

Prolog	*User*
?-	find_enemy.
Please enter the name of an animal	I will then tell
	you the name of the natural enemy
¦:	deer.
wolf	. . . (session ends)

Notice how we have now introduced another dimension to the program in that it now tells the user what he or she has to do to obtain the required information. The only restriction is that it can be awkward to have single quotes as part of the text, so words like don't are problematic.

As our enemy program stands at the moment the answer from the system is a little terse. We get the answer in the form **wolf**, whereas it would be much more pleasant if the system replied "the natural enemy of the deer is the wolf". This enhancement poses no problems, we just have to change the **find_enemy** rule slightly as follows.

```
find_enemy: - screen (['Please enter the name of the animal.',
'I will then tell you the name of the natural enemy']),
        read (X),
        enemy (X, Y),
        screen (['the natural enemy of the ']),
        write (X),
        screen ([' is the ']),
        write (Y).
```

Here is the program in operation

Prolog	*User*
?–	find_enemy.
Please enter the name of an animal.	I will then tell
	you the name of the natural enemy
¦:	deer.
the natural enemy of the deer is the wolf	
	. . . (session ends)

5.3 Exercise 11

Write a program that will accept the name of a calendar month and tell the
user what season of the year the month falls in.

5.4 Some more system predicates

5.4.1 The nl predicate

This predicate takes no arguments and the name of it is the initial letters of
'new line'. There are often occasions, when writing interactive routines, when
it is desirable to be able to space output in order to make it more readable. New
line **nl** causes subsequent output to begin on a new line and can, for example,
be used n conjunction with the **write** predicate. By way of an example let us
see how we could modify our screen predicate to output a user menu on to
the screen.

```
screen ([ ]) :- !.
screen ([H¦T]) :- write (H), nl, screen (T).

user_menu :- screen ([
'    This is an example of how Prolog can be',
' used to output large quantities of textual information',
' ',
'The top level user menu is shown below. Please enter your choice and
follow it with a full stop.',
' ',
' ',
```

```
 ,
 ,
 ,                                                             ,
 ,                                                             ,
 ,    ┌────────────────────────────────────────────────┐      ,
 ,    │                 USER MENU                       │      ,
 ,    ├────────────────────────────────────────────────┤      ,
 ,    │      ENTER 1 FOR SOMETHING OLD                  │      ,
 ,    │      ENTER 2 FOR SOMETHING NEW                  │      ,'
```

```
,  |          ENTER 3 FOR SOMETHING BORROWED          |  , '
,  |          ENTER 4 FOR SOMETHING BLUE              |  , '
'  |--------------------------------------------------|  , '
,  | ENTER YOUR CHOICE . . . . . . . .                |  , '
,  |_____|  , '
,                                                         , '
                                                      ]).
```

The screen predicate will now cause each element of the list to be output to
the screen, each starting on a new line. To obtain a blank line two new line
statements would have to be used, unless a special procedure for spacing such
as the one below were to be defined

throw (∅) :-!.
throw (N) :- nl, R is N−1, throw (R).

This is a useful spacing procedure in that N is set to the number of space lines
required for the text output; for example, **throw (3)** gives the equivalent of **nl**
being invoked 3 times.

5.4.2 The *tab* predicate

This can be used in a similar way to **nl**, to format text output. The predicate
takes one argument which must be instantiated to an integer value and it causes
the number of space characters specified by the integer to be output. If for
example you wanted to place a space either side of a name, **tab** could be used
as follows

tab (1), write (fred), tab (1).

5.4.3 The *get and get∅* predicates

These predicates are used to access single characters from the input terminal. The
difference between them is that **get** operates only on printing characters (those
that can be made to appear on the screen or printer (ASCII codes 32 or
greater)), whereas **get∅** can operate on any ASCII character. Both take a single
argument. If the argument is instantiated then the goal **get (X)** (or **get∅ (X)**)
succeeds if the next input character matches that argument and fails if it does
not. If the argument is not instantiated, that is **get (X)** or **get∅ (X)**, then the
argument is instantiated to the value of the next character input.
   Both **get** and **get∅** can only succeed once and cannot be resatisfied. Furthermore, they work on the ASCII code of the character, not the character as it

appears to the system user. A list of ASCII codes and corresponding characters is given in appendix 3. Here are three examples of these predicates in use

Prolog	*User*
?-	get (X).
¦:	a
X = 97	
?-	get∅ (1∅1).
¦:	a
no	
?-	get∅ (98).
¦:	b
yes	. . . (session ends)

The points to note are as follows. Firstly, the **get** and **get∅** predicates cause the system to wait for input when the system user is directly interacting with Prolog. In this respect they are similar to the **read** predicate. Secondly, the predicates deal with ASCII codes, not the characters that they represent. For example the ASCII codes of a and b are 97 and 98 respectively. Also no full stop is required after the character. This is because the full stop is itself a character and the two predicates require only one character for their argument.

There are many ways in which **get** and **get∅** can be used. As with all Prolog features, the best thing is to experiment with them and adapt their attributes for your own purposes.

5.4.4 The **put** predicate

The **put** predicate allows the output of a character to the screen. Like **get** and **get∅**, it takes one argument and succeeds only once. The argument (the ASCII code of the character you want to output) must be instantiated before **put** can succeed. It can be used in conjunction with **get** to echo characters on to the screen.

```
?-get (X), put (X).
¦:a
a
X = 97
```

In the above example the character **a** is input in response to the prompt generated by calling **get (X)**. **X** is then instantiated to **97** (the ASCII code of a) and calling **put (97)** results in the character **a** being output. Here is another example which shows how a lower case letter may be echoed to the screen as a capital letter.

	Prolog	*User*
	?-	get(X), Y is X − 32, put(Y).
	!:	a
	A	
	X = 97	
	Y = 65	

                                    . . . (session ends)

5.4.5 The *name* predicate

The name predicate can be used to convert ASCII characters to their character equivalents and vice versa. It takes two arguments, the second of which is represented to the system as a list.

There are a variety of uses for the name predicate and here are a few examples of it in operation

    ?-name (a, L).
    L = [97]

    ?- name (X, [97, 98, 99]).
    X = abc

    ?- name (abc, List).
    List = [97, 98, 99]

As you can see from the above examples it is possible to use the **name** predicate to convert the ASCII representation of characters obtained using **get** and **get0** to their normal character representation.

5.5 Exercise 12

Write a program to carry out the following

(i) Read a word from the input terminal, which is not terminated by a full stop (therefore you cannot use **read**), but has the end of the word signalled by the input of carriage return.

(ii) Output a sentence to the terminal of the format

   "the word just read was . . . as you can see"

inserting your word in place of the full stops.

Hints: Use **get0** to read the word character by character (the ASCII code for carriage return is 13), and use the **name** predicate to convert from ASCII to character format.

5.6 Getting Prolog to 'learn'

Although there are many uses for the facilities to be described in this section, they are of great use in the area of interactive programming. An interactive system becomes much more powerful if it can remember what has been said to it. Furthermore, it is necessary on occasions to have the system 'forget' what it has been told. Prolog provides us with the ability to tell the system what it needs to remember and what it needs to forget. Of course, this is a long way removed from the full meaning of the word 'learn' (hence the inverted commas) but it is certainly a necessary part of the learning process and represents an essential building block for intelligent systems.

5.6.1 The *assert* predicate

This predicate takes one argument which must be instantiated to a clause. The effect of **assert (X)** is to place the clause instantiated to **X** in the knowledge base. Furthermore, it has two additional formats which provide more control over where the clause is placed in the knowledge base.

asserta (X) — places the clause instantiated to **X** before any other clauses of the same predicate and number of arguments in the knowledge base.

assertz (X) — places the clause instantiated to **X** after any other clauses of the same predicate and number of arguments in the knowledge base.

These predicates therefore allow us to add to the knowledge base, in other words to remember additional information. Once an **assert** goal has been satisfied, the clause remains in the knowledge base until it is removed. Here is a simple example

Prolog	User
?-	asserta (man (john)).
yes ?-	man (X).
X = john	. . . (session ends)

As you can see, the clause **man (john)** has been added to the knowledge base and is immediately available for use thereafter.

Let us take another example. Suppose we wish the system to remember the name of the system user. We could program as follows

```
introduce:-screen (['Hello what is your name']),
          remember.
remember :-read (X), assertz (user_name (X)).
```

    screen ([ ]): - !
    screen ([H T]): - write (H), nl, screen (T).

Here is the program in use

Prolog	User
?-	introduce
Hello what is your name	
¦:	jim.
?-	user_name (X).
X = jim	

Although **asserta** and **assertz** take only one argument, the clause that represents that argument can be complex. All these are valid assertions

    asserta (group (birds, [eagle, finch, canary])).
    assertz (worker (surname (jones), initial (p))).
    assertz ((go:- test (X), write (Y))).

We will return to the use of **assert** presently, but first we will discuss the use of the predicate that allows the program to 'forget'.

5.6.2 *The* **retract** *predicate*

This also takes one argument, again instantiated to a clausal form, but its effect is to remove clauses from the knowledge base. Once a **retract** goal has succeeded, the clause referred to is lost from the knowledge base. Here is an example

Prolog	User
?-	asserta (man (john)).
yes	
?-	man (X).
X = john	
yes	
?-	retract (man (john)).
yes	
?-	man (X).
no	. . . (session ends)

In the above example we have retracted a clause which has both the predicate and argument named, that is, **man** and **john**. However it is possible to use **retract** in the situation where only the predicate is named. For example, **retract (man (X))**. In that situation Prolog will remove the first clause it encounters with the predicate **man** and one argument. Any further clauses of the same predicate and same number of arguments require **retract** to be resatisfied before they can be removed. For example

Prolog	User
?–	asserta (man (john)).
yes	
?–	assertz (man (fred)).
yes	
?–	man (X).
X = john	;
X = fred	;
yes	
?–	retract (man (X)).
X = john	
yes	
?–	man (X).
X = fred	;
no	. . . (session ends)

As you can see, the **retract** predicate removed only the first assertion of **man**.
You might also care to note that had the second man, **fred**, been entered using
asserta, he would have been placed first in the knowledge base and would have
been removed by **retract (man (X))**.

5.7 Generating multiple solutions inside the program

5.7.1 The **fail** predicate

There are many practical programming situations where it is not convenient
for alternative solutions to be invoked by typing in the semi-colon ; prompt.
There is a technique available to us which can allow us to force the program to
backtrack even when it has successfully generated a goal solution. This process
is based on the system predicate **fail**, which always fails.
Here is an example of the **fail** predicate in use

```
read_sentence (X) :– read (X), !, entry (W, X), test (W).
test (yes) :– write ('word "yes" identified').
test (_): – fail.
entry (W, [W|_]).
entry (W, [_|T]) :– entry (W, T).
```

In the above example we are reading in a sentence input as a list, identifying
each word in it (using **entry** as defined in chapter 4) and seeing whether the
word is **yes** — if it is we carry out a procedure to write a message to the user,
if it is not we want to go back and see whether or not the next word in the
sentence is **yes**. Should the word **yes** not be present at all we want the procedure to fail. It would be tedious for the user to have to continually prompt
for the process to be repeated and so we use **fail** to ensure that the program is
forced to backtrack until it finds the word **yes**.

First let us see the program working and then analyse what is happening

Prolog	*User*
?-	read_sentence (X).
!:	[please, say, yes].
X = [please, say, yes]	
word "yes" identified	. . . (session ends)

This is what has happened to provide the above result:

(1) When the read instruction is encountered, that is, the first sub-goal of **read_sentence,** the program stops and gives a prompt for the input — that is supplied in the form of the sentence entered as a list.

(2) The second sub-goal of **read_sentence** is the cut and we will return to that presently; at the moment the cut succeeds and we pass on to the third sub-goal.

(3) The third sub-goal, **entry**, successfully establishes the word **please** as a word in the sentence and **W** is instantiated to **please** and passed to the next sub-goal, **test.**

(4) The first clause of **test** fails because the word does not have the value **yes.** Therefore an attempt is made to succeed with the second clause of **test** and that will succeed for any value of **W.** Thus the sub-goal **fail** fails but the effect of **fail** failing is for **read_sentence** to fail and backtracking now takes place. Therefore another attempt to succeed with **entry** takes place which results in **W** being instantiated to **say.**

(5) Events (3) and (4) are now repeated until the third word **yes** is identified. This time **fail** is not reached and the **read_sentence** goal has succeeded.

(6) The cut is placed after the **read** sub-goal in the body of the **read_sentence** rule to prevent the program running indefinitely should the word **yes** not be input. The way in which it operates is to prevent an attempt to backtrack to the sub-goal **read** if the sentence does not contain **yes.** Were the cut not present the program would prompt for new sentences to be input until the word **yes** were recognised.

5.7.2 The **true** predicate

We have seen above that it is possible to have a procedure which 'fails' under all conditions. The system predicate **true** provides the opposite; it succeeds under all conditions.

5.7.3 The **repeat** predicate

The predicate **repeat** always succeeds and can be used to generate an infinite sequence of choices. Once the predicate has succeeded on backtracking, the execution of clauses after **repeat** in the rule body continues as if they were being executed for the first time, that is, as if no backtracking had taken place.

To make it clear how the **repeat** predicate works, consider the following knowledge base and terminal session.

>   tailor (jones).
>   tailor (smith).
>   tailor (brown).
>   g (X) :- repeat, tailor (X).
>   f (X) :- tailor (X).

Prolog	User
?-	f (X)
X = jones	;
X = smith	;
X = brown	;
no ?-	g (X).
X = jones	;
X = smith	;
X = brown	;
X = jones	;
X = smith	
. .	
. .	. . . (session ends)

As you can see, **f (X)** has three solutions which are elicited by enforcing backtracking using the ; prompt. However we can see that when the repeat predicate is encountered on backtracking it succeeds and allows Prolog to start searching the knowledge base from the top again. In so doing it allows an infinite number of solutions to be generated, even though some of them may be duplicated as we have seen here.

5.7.4 Negation

During the normal flow of a program, Prolog will only attempt to satisfy a later clause in the body of a rule if the previous goals can be proved true (either directly from assertions in the database or by inference from those assertions). For example, to prove the rule for **alpha** shown below, the goals **b**, **c**, **d** and **e** would have to be proved true.

>   alpha:-b, c, d, e.

However, it may be more convenient for us to specify a goal in the body of a rule as being true if some assertion or inference from assertions is not true. Referring to the following database

> citrus_fruit (X) :- lemon (X).
> citrus_fruit (X) :- orange (X).
> orange (seville)
> lemon (lemon).

let us now write a rule to specify a sweet fruit, that is, a fruit that is not a citrus fruit. We could write something like

> sweet_fruit (X) :- citrus_fruit (X), !, fail.
> sweet_fruit (_).

Here the first rule will fail if **X** is a citrus fruit and allow no backtracking to find other solutions (the inclusion of the cut prevents this). If **X** is not a citrus fruit then the second clause will succeed. This is a rather cumbersome way of performing negation and most Prolog implementations will provide a system predicate that performs negation. On the DEC-10 the predicate is **\+(X)**, but on some other versions of Prolog (see the appendixes) the predicate used is **not (X)**, where **X** in both cases is an assertion in the database or the head of a rule. The goal defined by these negative forms succeeds if the clause which represents the argument to the negation is not provable. So our definition for a sweet fruit may now become

> sweet_fruit (X) :-\+ (citrus_fruit (X)).

5.8 Solutions to exercises

Exercise 11

> go:-screen ([
>   'Please enter the name of a calendar month",
>   'I will tell you which season it falls in']),
>   read (X), find_season (Y, X), output (X, Y).
>
> find_season (Y, X) :- season (Y, W), entry (X, W).
> output (X, Y) :- screen ([
>   ' ',
>   ' The month of ', X,' falls in the season of',
>   Y]).
> entry (A, [A|_]).
> entry (A, [_|L]) :- entry (A, L).

```
screen ([]) :- !
screen ([H¦T]) :- write (H), write (' '), screen (T).
season (winter, [november, december, january, february]).
season (spring, [march, april, may]).
season (summer, [june, july, august]).
season (autumn, [september, october]).
```

The program is invoked by the question **go**.

Exercise 12

```
go :- go ([]).
go (Y) :- get0 (X),
          concatenate (X, Y, Z), !,
          (X = 13; go (Z)),
          reverse_list (Z, R),
          name (V, R),
          write (' The word entered was '),
          write (V),
          write (' as you can see'), !, fail.

reverse_list ([], []).
reverse_list ([H¦T], P) :- reverse_list (T, Q),
                                  concatenate (Q, [H], P).
concatenate ([], X, X).
concatenate ([H¦X], Y, [H¦Z]) :- concatenate (X, Y, Z).
```

The program is started by asking the question **go**. which causes the recursive definition of **go** to be entered. The recursion is terminated when carriage return (ASCII code 13) is entered.

6 More Advanced Programming Tools

In the first five chapters, we have described the features of Prolog which are necessary to allow us to produce working interactive programs. The language has been used only to provide direct interaction between user and terminal. In fact, Prolog provides comprehensive stream and file handling facilities and for serious system development these will almost always be utilised in one way or another.

In addition to that, there are other language features which we have not yet mentioned which allow the programming of more complex processes. Our intention is to use chapters 6, 7 and 8 to introduce the more sophisticated facilities of the language in as straightforward a manner as possible. As with any programming language, there is no better way to learn than to experiment with the language features and learn about them in a practical manner. If that involves making a few mistakes it is no great tragedy!

As we have already seen, Prolog implementations contain a selection of system predicates, which handle operations such as input/output, arithmetic and program control. In this chapter we will look at some more system predicates, as well as revisiting some familiar predicates and discussing them in more detail.

6.1 Predicates for input and output

We have seen that for a Prolog program to communicate with the outside world it must have input and output capabilities. You should already be familiar with the input and output of information between the program and your terminal. This is a special case of the input and output mechanisms that Prolog supports. Prolog communicates with your terminal by treating it as if it were a file, which it is able to write to and read from. Your terminal is designated as the 'USER' file and if no other file is specified all input and output will take place with this file. In general, Prolog will always read from the *current* input stream and write to the *current* output stream. On the DEC-10 Prolog (version 3.47) a total of fourteen I/O streams may be open at any one time, but input and output will take place only on the current stream, which is not the same as an open stream.

To open a file for reading or writing we must first inform the Prolog system that the file is about to become the current input or output stream. We can do this using the clauses **see (X)** and **tell (X)** respectively. If the system predicate **see** is used we are saying that we want to treat the contents of file **X** as input, Thus if a **see** instruction is followed by a **read** instruction the first term in the file referenced by **see** is read. If **X** is not instantiated or is instantiated to a filename that does not exist an error will occur. Similarly if we use **tell (X)** we are saying that we want to treat file **X** as the current output stream. As with the system predicate **see**, the argument must be instantiated. However if the argument is instantiated to a filename that does not exist a file of that name is created. If the argument is instantiated to a filename that already exists then the contents of the original file will be destroyed. For example if we wish to read from the file '**Fred. txt**' we would use the predicate **see (X)** with **X** instantiated to '**Fred. txt**', thus

    see ('Fred. txt').

Notice that **X** must be atomic, so the filename is enclosed in quotes.

We have seen how it is possible to open new input and output streams and alter the current output streams using the clauses **see (X)** and **tell (X)**. To close the current input and output streams the predicates **seen** and **told** are used respectively. The clause **close (X)** may also be used, which closes the file **X** for both input and output. So a simple example using these predicates would be

    open_and_close (X, Y) :–see (X), tell (Y), process, seen, told.

where **process** is a predicate that defines some operation using files **X** and **Y**.

If at any time we wish to know which file is on the current input or output stream, the clauses **seeing (X)** and **telling (X)** may be used respectively. The variable **X** will be instantiated to the file name in both cases.

Now that we can control the assignment of the current input and output streams we are ready to begin reading and writing characters and terms (an atom, integer, variable or structure) on these data streams.

6.1.1 Character input output

The system predicates used for character input output can be split into two groups, those for use on the current stream and those for use on the user stream. Notice that the predicates used for writing to the current stream can be used for writing to the terminal providing the terminal is the current stream (that is, the user stream). This is in fact how we have used the current stream predicates in previous chapters.

Current stream predicates

The clauses **get0 (X)**, **get (X)**, **put (X)**, **tab (X)** and **nl** all act in the same way as they did in chapter 5, however we know that they now operate on the current stream. (In chapter 5 the user stream was the current stream.)

Another useful predicate is the **skip** predicate which takes one argument and reads and skips over characters on the current input stream until a character on the stream matches with its argument. It succeeds only once and cannot be resatisfied.

Terminal (USER) stream predicates

All of the predicates listed below have the same effect as the more general predicates described previously which are not preceded by **tty**, except that they refer only to the user stream no matter what the current stream is set to. For example, **ttynl** writes a new line to the user stream, whereas **nl** writes a new line to the current output stream, which may of course be the user stream. The predicates are used as follows

ttynl	**ttyget0 (X)**	**ttyget (X)**
ttyskip (X)	**ttyput (X)**	**ttytab (X)**

An additional predicate that may be used on the user stream is **ttyflush**. Output to the terminal using either **ttyput (X)** or **put (X)** usually goes into an output buffer until a new line is output. Calling this predicate causes any characters in the buffer to be output immediately.

You have now been introduced to the system predicates Prolog has for dealing with characters on both the current and user streams. Let us look at a simple example of some of the above predicates at work.

Example

Suppose that we have a problem where it is necessary to create two separate files, merge them together into a single file and then output the merged file to the user's terminal. We could proceed using the following program.

```
process (X, Y, Z) :- create_file (X, Y),
                     merge (X, Y, Z),
                     read_write (Z).
create_file (X, Y) :- writefile (X), writefile (Y).
writefile (X) :- tell (X), repeat, get0 (N),
                 (eof (N) ; put (N)), eof (N), told.
eof (26).
eof (36).
merge (X, Y, Z) :- tell (Z), read_write (X), read_write (Y), told.
read_write (X) :- see (X), repeat, get0 (N),
                  (eof (N) ; put (N)), eof (N), seen.
```

The predicate **process** forms the general description of our problem. That is we create the two files, merge them and output the result to the user stream. The files **X** and **Y** are the names of the two files we create which are then merged to form the file **Z**. The end of file input for the files **S** and **Y** is signified by detecting the $ character on the current input stream (ASCII 36), using the clause **eof (N)**. The end of file when reading files is signified by the ^**Z** character (ASCII 26).

Here is a terminal session using the program.

Prolog	*User*
?–	**process ('File1', 'File2', 'File3').**
¦:	**hello $**
¦:	**there !$**
hello there !	
?–	. . . (session ends)

6.1.2 *Input and output of terms*

In this section we describe the predicates that may be used to input and output Prolog terms. You should already be familiar with the predicates **read** and **write** but we will mention them again to reinforce the material we covered using them in chapter 5.

write (X)   The term instantiated to **X** is written to the current output stream.

read (X)   The next term on the current input stream is read in and assigned to **X**. Note that the term must be delimited by a full stop followed by a space or control character. The delimiting full stop does not become part of the term and is removed from the current input stream. (You may remember from the previous chapter that when you were inputting terms using read you had to follow each term with a full stop and carriage return.) If an invocation of **read (X)** causes the end of file character to be reached, then **X** will be instantiated to the term **end_of_file**. If a further invocation of **read (X)** is attempted then an error will occur.

display (X)   The term to which **X** is instantiated is displayed on the terminal (user stream), ignoring any operator declarations (see section 6.5). If **X** is a structure then its predicate is printed first followed by its arguments in parentheses. Note that the user stream does not have to be the current stream.

writeq (X)   The term that **X** is instantiated to is written to the current output stream according to the current operator declarations. However the names of the atoms are quoted where necessary to make the result

acceptable to the system predicate **read** discussed earlier. Thus for
example **writeq ('KKK')** will result in **'KKK'** being output to
the current output stream whereas **write ('KKK')** will result in **KKK**
being output on the current output stream. This is important if
you are writing data to a file.

6.2 Modifying the database

When you are using Prolog you will probably find that situations will arise where
you will want to alter the contents of the database. We have already used the
predicates **assert, asserta, assertz** and **retract** to modify the database. If we have
a large number of clauses to add or remove from the database, using the predicates listed above can become rather cumbersome.

6.2.1 The **abolish** predicate

If you wish to retract all the clauses for a particular predicate you could use
retract on all the clauses of that name in the database. However an easier method
is to use the clause **abolish (X, Y)**, which removes all the clauses with predicate
X and arity **Y** from the database. For example supposing we have the following
knowledge base

> **finance (john, manager, senior).**
> **finance (fred, clerk).**

then the goal

> **abolish (finance, 3).**

will remove the assertion **finance (john, manager, senior)**. Correspondingly if
the goal **abolish (finance, 2)** was set, the clause **finance (fred, clerk)** would be
removed from the knowledge base.

Here is a user-defined predicate **retractall** which performs a similar function.

> **retractall (X) :– retract (X), fail.**
> **retractall (_).**

6.2.2 Altering the database using files

There are two predicates provided to handle the modification of the database
using files. These are **consult** and **reconsult**, taking a single argument which is
the name of a text file containing Prolog clauses. The clause **consult (X)**
causes the Prolog interpreter to read in clauses from the file **X** (you will
probably remember this because it is used to input your program). However it
is worth noting that if you already have clauses in the knowledge base, the effect

of **consult (X)** is to insert clauses from the file **X** into the knowledge base such that clauses with a name identical to clauses already in the knowledge base will appear at the end of the set of clauses with that procedure name. The predicate **reconsult** works in a similar manner to the **consult** predicate, except that it removes from the original knowledge base any clauses that have the same name and arity as those being added. To clarify the operation of **consult** and **reconsult** consider the following example.

Example

Suppose that we have two files '**pre.pro**' and '**post.pro**' containing the clauses shown below.

file: 'pre.pro'

```
make (ford).
make (vauxhall).
make (british_leyland).
engine ('2 litre').
engine ('3.5 litre').
engine ('1.6 litre').
model (escort) :- engine ('1.6 litre'),
                  make (ford).
model (rover) :- engine ('3.5 litre'),
                 make (british_leyland).
```

file: 'post.pro'

```
make (ford).
engine ('2 litre').
model (sierra) :- engine ('2 litre'),
                  model (ford).
```

If we load in the file '**pre.pro**' as our initial knowledge base using **consult ('pre. pro')**, the effect of consulting or reconsulting the file '**post.pro**' is shown below. Notice that the filename is quoted in order to make it atomic.

Using **consult ('post.pro')** the knowledge base would become

```
make (ford).
make (vauxhall).
make (british_leyland).
make (ford).
engine ('2 litre').
engine ('3.5 litre').
engine ('1.6 litre').
engine ('2 litre').
```

model (escort) :- engine ('1.6 litre'),
                  make (ford).
model (rover) :- engine ('3.5 litre'),
                 make (british_leyland).
model (sierra) :- engine ('2 litre'),
                  make (ford).

If **reconsult** (`'post.pro'`) were used then the knowledge base would become

make (ford).
engine ('2 litre').
model (sierra) :- engine ('2 litre'),
                  make (ford).

The predicates **consult** and **reconsult** may be used as part of a clause, such that new files can be input while the program is running. Alternatively the predicates can be used at the top level of the Prolog interpreter, that is when the system prompt is showing.

6.3 Meta logical predicates

The meta logical predicates provided are a set of system predicates that are concerned with Prolog terms in the knowledge base. They are used to test for certain characteristics and to manipulate the terms. Some of the predicates provided are given below, along with a brief description of their operation.

ancestors   This predicate takes a single argument and instantiates it
                   to a list which contains all the ancestor goals for the current
                   clause. The ancestors of a goal are those goals by which it
                   is called as a sub-goal. For example, suppose we have the
                   following knowledge base

size (14).
find_size (X) :- try_size (X).
try_size (X) :- size (X),
                ancestors (Y),
                write (Y).

Then the question **find_size (X)** will instantiate **Y** to the list [**try_size (14)**, **find_size (14)**] and **X** to **14**. The current clause in this case is **size (X)**; it is the clause previous to the call to **ancestors (Y)**.

var (X)   Succeeds if **X** is a variable. For example

?-var (_125).
yes

      ?–var (alan).
      no

nonvar (X)   Succeeds if **X** is not a variable.

atom (X)   Succeeds if **X** is an atom (a non-variable term of arity zero). For example

      ?–atom (alan).
      yes
      ?–atom (male(alan)).
      no

integer (X)   Succeeds if **X** is instantiated to an integer.

atomic (X)   Succeeds if **X** is instantiated to an atom or an integer.

arg (X, Y, Z)   The system predicate **arg** is one of a group of predicates that allow the structure and content of Prolog clauses to be examined. As you can see it takes three arguments. The first represents the particular argument of a clause in which we are interested, the second represents the clause and the third represents the value of the argument so defined. For example

      ?–arg (1, married (john, jane), john).
      yes
      ?–arg (2, append ([ ] , a, [a]), X).
      X = a
      yes
      ?–read (X), arg (1, X, A).
      ¦:'controls (security, system_a, condition_red)'.
      X = controls (security, system_a, condition_red)
      A=security.

functor (X, Y, A)   This system predicate takes three arguments and is also useful for analysing the structure of Prolog clauses. The first argument represents the clause, the second the predicate or operator representing the functor of the clause and the third the arity of the clause. For example

      ?–functor (supervises (smith, brown), X, 2).
      X=supervises
      ?–functor (is_a (hall, lecturer), is_a, 2).
      yes

T=. .L   This is a useful Prolog feature which enables us to transform

a clause into a list or vice versa. In the example below it is
used to turn a statement in English into a Prolog goal

```
build_goal (L, T) :- read (L),
                     entry (V, L),
                     verb (V),
                     entry (N1, L),
                     noun (N1),
                     entry (N2, L),
                     \+ (N2=N1),
                     append ([ ], V.L1),
                     append (L1, N1, L2),
                     append (L2, N2, L3),
                     T= . .L3.
entry (E, [E¦_]).
entry (E, [_¦T]) :- entry (E, T).
append ([ ], E, [E]).
append ([H¦X], E, [H¦Y]) :- append (X, E, Y).
verb (knows).
noun (alison).
noun (prolog).

?-build_goal (L, T).
¦: [alison, knows, prolog].
L=[alison, knows, prolog]
T = knows (alison, prolog)
```

length (L, N)   This predicate instantiates the variable **N** to the number of
                   elements in the list **L**.

call (X)   This predicate executes the goal **X**. It has the same function
                   as asking the question **X** of the knowledge base. For example

        call (man (Y)).

6.4 Performing logical tests

The following predicates (operators) are used to perform comparative tests on
Prolog terms, in much the same way as the comparative operators used in
arithmetic in Prolog.

X == Y The == operator tests to see if the terms **X** and **Y** are identical (including the names of variables). For example the test

        apple (X) == apple (X)

will succeed, whereas the test

apple (X) == apple (Y)

will fail because the variable names are not identical.

X \== Y Tests to see that the terms **X** and **Y** are not identical. Thus the test

apple (X) \== apple (Y)

will succeed, and the test

apple (X) \== apple (X)

will fail.

X = Y Tests to see that the terms instantiated to **X** and **Y** are equal. If either **X** or **Y** are uninstantiated then the one is instantiated to the other. Notice the difference between the = operator and the == operator. The goal **X = Y** will succeed, whereas the goal **X == Y** will fail.

X \= Y Tests to see that the terms **X** and **Y** are not equal.

6.5 Operators

Imagine that you wish to write down an expression that represents the addition of the integers 2 and 3. You would probably write down 2 + 3. This is the shorthand way of writing the expression described above. What you have actually done is defined an operator + that represents the addition of the integers 2 and 3. You now know what an operator is and the function it performs. However, there are several different categories of operator that may be defined. These are prefix, postfix and infix operators. A prefix operator is placed before its argument, a postfix operator is placed after its argument and an infix operator is placed between its arguments. Some examples are given below.

Prefix operators
−3   +4 $7

Infix operators
2 + 3   A & B

Postfix operators
3!   3j   4%

Although we have considered the position of an operator in relation to its arguments this is not enough to completely specify it. We must also consider the question of *associativity* between the operator and its arguments as well as the *precedence* of the operator.

6.5.1 Operator precedence

The precedence of an operator tells us which operations to perform first. For example, given the expression

2 + 3/5

you would probably obtain the answer of 2.6. This is because when you were taught mathematics you were told that the operations of multiplication and division have to be performed before those of addition and subtraction. In order to ensure that the operations of multiplication and division are performed before those of addition and subtraction they are assigned a lower precedence number. You may however decide to define your arithmetical functions such that addition is performed before multiplication by assigning the operator for addition a lower precedence number than that for multiplication. Clearly, when we assign the precedence of an operator we have to think carefully of the order in which the operations are to occur. The precedence of an operator is defined by assigning it an integer number. The range will depend on the implementation you are using (for the DEC-10 the range is 1 to 1200). The higher the integer assigned to an operator the greater the precedence of that operator.

6.5.2 Operator associativity

There are several possibilities for specifying the associativity of the operators.
The possible specifications for infix operators are

xfx   xfy   yfx

and those for prefix and postfix operators are

xf   yf   fx   fy

where

> **f** is the operator.
> **x** specifies that any operator in the argument **x** must have a lower precedence number than the operator **f**.
> **y** specifies that the argument **y** can contain operators which have equal or lower precedence numbers than the operator **f**.

Example

Suppose we define the multiplication operator ∗, and division operator / as having associativity **yfx** and equal precedence, then the expression

    3∗4/5

is evaluated as

    (3∗4) / 5

not

    3 ∗ (4/5)

Notice that the **x** specifier is the one which allows the meaning of a possibly ambiguous expression to be resolved, since the **x** terms must always have a lower precedence than the operator **f**.

6.5.3 Defining operators

The system predicate **op (X, Y, Z)** is used to define the operator **Z**, where **Y** is the associativity of the operator **Z**, and **X** is the precedence. For example, the following operator definition could be used to define the addition operator **+**

    :–op (2∅∅, yfx, +).

If you should wish to define several operators of the same precedence and associativity, **Z** may be a list containing those operators. For example

    :–op (2∅∅, yfx, [+, -, &]).

Let us now look at a simple example using an operator to define the factorial operation

```
:–op (3∅∅, xf, '!').
N! :– factorial (N, Y), screen (N, Y).
factorial (∅, 1).
factorial (N, Y) :–M is N–1, factorial (M, G), Y is N∗G.
screen (N, Y) :–write (N), write (' ! is'), write (Y).
```

An example of the above program in use is given below

Prolog	*User*
?–	**4!.**
4 ! is 24	
?–	**. . . (session ends).**

6.6 The Prolog high-level grammar syntax

This syntax is an interesting and useful addition to the Prolog language because
it facilitates one of the applications to which Prolog is best suited, that is,
natural language processing. Case study 2 given in chapter 8 presents an
example of the high-level syntax at work, where it is used in conjunction with a
sentence-reading routine (based on a program presented in *How to solve it with
Prolog* by Helder Coelho, Jose Carlos Cotta and Luis Moniz Pereizo (Labora-
toria Nactional de Engenhasia Civil, Lisboa, Portugal)) to read sentences in
English into the system and classify them. Although the program has no direct
application it does form the basis of a much larger system which uses natural
language to interface to an Expert Resource Management System (the system is
considered much too complex to present as a case study).

The high-level grammar syntax is translated by the Prolog system into Prolog
rules and assertions, but it is more convenient to work at the higher level. You
should note that not all Prolog implementations support this feature (those
that do may vary slightly in their method of implementation, you should consult
your User Manual for further details). The examples and discussion used here
and in the case study are consistent with the grammar syntax present on the
Quintus Prolog implementation.

6.6.1 Defining a grammar

If you look at case study 2 you will find specific examples of the grammar
syntax at work. However we will start at a fairly simple level by examining
the sentence

    "the lecturer bores the students"

As you can see this is a very simple sentence, but we could break it down
into a noun phrase

    "the lecturer"

followed by a verb phrase

    "bores the students"

The noun phrase then breaks down into a determiner "the" and a noun "man". The verb phrase parses as a verb "eats" and a noun phrase "the meal".

Using sentences with the above simple structure as a basis, we can construct a grammar that can deal with them as follows

> **sentence** ⟶ **np, vp.**
> **np** ⟶ **det, noun.**
> **vp** ⟶ **verb, np.**

Having constructed our simple grammar we must now provide a simple vocabulary, in this instance an extremely small one.

> **det** ⟶ [**the**].
> **noun** ⟶ [**lecturer**].
> **noun** ⟶ [**students**]
> **verb** ⟶ [**bores**].

We have now constructed a system that will recognise any valid sentence constructed from the words in the vocabulary. The ⟶ operator means consists of, and the , operator means followed by. Thus taking the first grammar rule we can see that a sentence consists of a noun phrase followed by a verb phrase. Case study 2 take this idea a little further.

6.6.2 *The phrase predicate*

This is an extremely useful predicate for checking the validity of a given phrase according to the grammar. For example if we set the goal

> **phrase (sentence, [the, lecturer, bores, the, students]).**

the goal will succeed using the above grammar and vocabulary. Similarly, the goals

> **phrase (np, [the, lecturer]).**
> **phrase (vp, [bores, the, students]).**

will also succeed, but the goals

> **phrase (np, [bores, students]).**
> **phrase (vp, [plays, the, piano]).**

will both fail, in the first instance because the structure conflicts with the grammar rules and in the second because, although the statement is in fact a verb phrase, the words "plays" and "piano" are not in the programmed vocabulary. An interesting experiment you can try is to define a simple grammar and a small vocabulary and set the goal

phrase (sentence, X).

The system will generate all possible combinations of words in the vocabulary that constitute sentences according to the defined grammar. Be warned however; keep the vocabulary small because immense numbers of valid sentences may be generated from comparatively few words.

You will probably have noticed by now that the grammar handles language structures in the form of lists. This makes a lot of sense because data structures such as "the lecturer bores the students" are unsuitable for all applications other than unintelligent "string handling" operations. Clearly, for serious processing we need a structure that lends itself to the identification and analysis of significant language elements. Lists are excellent for this purpose. Firstly because they allow us to handle the whole sentence as a single argument, and secondly because we can address individual list elements, by means of list manipulation predicates such as those described in chapter 4.

Although the case study uses the grammar syntax to process English sentences, there is no reason why it should be restricted to that context. An interesting idea is to use the grammar to interpret digital signals. Here is an example program written to do this.

```
signal ⟶ word, separator, extension.
word ⟶ digit, word_extension.
extension ⟶ signal.
extension ⟶ [ ].
word_extension ⟶ word.
word_extension ⟶ [ ].
separator ⟶ [s].
separator ⟶ [t].
digit ⟶ ['1'].
digit ⟶ ['∅'].
```

Using such a grammar, goals like

phrase (signal, [1, 1, ∅, 1, 1, 1, s, 1, 1, 1, s, ∅, ∅, 1, ∅, t]).
phrase (signal, [1, 1, ∅, ∅, 1, ∅, 1, 1, 1, t]).

will succeed. This type of idea has some interesting practical applications and a grammar of this type is currently being used in a robotics research project.

7 The Debugging Facility

These predicates are provided in order to enable the user to watch the flow of
the program, and hence remove any bugs that may be present. In order to
understand the discussion of the debugging predicates later in the chapter
you will find it helpful to be familiar with the "box model" for control flow
in a Prolog program, which is outlined below.

7.1 The box model

To explain the box model for control flow we first have to assume that every
Prolog procedure is contained inside an imaginary box. An example is given
below for the procedure **apple** and **concatenate**.

> **apple (X) :– object (X, round),**
> **colour (X, green).**

> **conc (A, [ ] , A).**
> **conc (A, [H¦T] , D) :– conc ([H¦A] , T, D).**

We now assume that the box is closed and that we may enter or leave the
box only under certain conditions. So under what circumstances will we want
to enter the box? Well, we will want to enter the box when we are trying to
satisfy goals that involve the clauses contained in the box. That is when we
invoke or call the procedure. A **CALL** label is therefore placed as an entrance
to the box as shown below with the procedure **conc**.

> CALL →
> **conc (A, [ ] , A).**
> **conc (A, [H¦T] , D) :–conc (H¦A] , T, D).**

This type of entry would take place when a call is made as an attempt to
satisfy part of a rule or as a direct request from the user's terminal. For example

> **?–conc ([a, b, c] , [d, e, f] , Y).**

Once we have entered the procedure box we have to try and satisfy the

83

procedure before we can attempt to get out of the box. As we know, when we try to satisfy the procedure we will either succeed and we will exit the procedure, or it will fail. To summarise, we leave the **EXIT** port of the box if the procedure call was successful and we leave the **FAIL** port if the attempt to satisfy the procedure was unsuccessful, as shown below.

```
CALL →    ┌─────────────────────────┐
          │       "procedure"        │ → EXIT
FAIL ←    └─────────────────────────┘
```

We must now cover the possibility that Prolog has previously satisfied the procedure but is forced to reconsider it by the failure of a subsequent goal. This option is provided by including a **REDO** port on the model as shown.

```
CALL →    ┌─────────────────────────┐   ← REDO
          │       "procedure"        │
FAIL ←    └─────────────────────────┘   → EXIT
```

We have now defined the basic box model, used to represent the control of the Prolog program.

To provide compatibility with the DEC-10 debugger we must also provide an invocation number and a number which represents the depth of invocation. The invocation number appears in parentheses on the debugging messages, and is a number assigned to a box when it is entered by the **CALL** port. The first box to be entered will be assigned an invocation number of 1, the second 2 and so on. Note that these boxes could be the same box called as part of a recursive procedure. Two examples are given below; the first shows how the box model works with a recursive procedure, the second shows how it works when backtracking takes place.

The depth of invocation number may be thought of as giving the number of rules that have to be satisfied, in order to prove the initial enquiry from the top level of the Prolog system. That is, it gives the number of ancestors of that particular goal. Referring to the examples, notice how the **conc** predicate has to prove 4 rules in order to satisfy the initial enquiry, whereas the **apple** predicate only needs to prove 1 rule.

Examples

The knowledge base is as follows

```
conc (A, [ ] , A).
conc (A, [H¦T] , D) :- conc ([H¦A] , T, D).
fruit (victoria_plum).
fruit (granny_smith).
shape (victoria_plum, round).
shape (granny_smith, round).
```

colour (victoria_plum, purple).
colour (granny_smith, green),
apple (X) :-fruit (X), shape (X, round), colour (X, green).

The following are the output from the debugger in response to the questions shown

?-conc ([a, b, c, d], [e, f, g, h], P).
(1) 0 Call : conc ([a, b, c, d], [e, f, g, h], _75)
(2) 1 Call: conc ([e, a, b, c, d], [f, g, h], _75)
(3) 2 Call : conc ([f, e, a, b, c, d], [g, h], _75)
(4) 3 Call : conc ([g, f, e, a, b, c, d], [h], _75)
(5) 4 Call : conc ([h. g. f. e. a. b, c, d], [], _75)
(5) 4 Call : conc ([h, g, f, e, a, b, c, d], [], [h, g, f, e, a, b, c, d])
(4) 3 Exit : conc ([g, f, e, a, b, c, d], [h], [h, g, f, e, a, b, c, d])
(3) 2 Exit : conc ([f, e, a, b, c, d], [g, h], [h, g, f, e, a, b, c, d])
(2) 1 Exit : conc ([e, a, b, c, d], [f, g, h], [h, g, f, e, a, b, c, d])
(1) 0 Exit : conc ([a, b, c, d], [e, f, g, h], [h, g, f, e, a, b, c, d])

p = [h, g, f, e, a, b, c, d]

(1) 0 Call : apple (_24)
(2) 1 Call : fruit (_24)
(2) 1 Exit : fruit (victoria_plum)
(3) 1 Call : shape (victoria_plum, round)
(3) 1 Exit : shape (victoria_plum, round)
(4) 1 Call : colour (victoria_plum, green)
(4) 1 Fail : colour (victoria_plum, green)
(3) 1 Redo : shape (victoria_plum, round)
(3) 1 Fail : shape (victoria_plum, round)
(2) 1 Redo : fruit (victoria_plum)
(2) 1 Exit : fruit (granny_smith)
(5) 1 Call : shape (granny_smith, round)
(5) 1 Exit : shape (granny_smith, round)
(6) 1 Exit : shape (granny_smith, round)
(6) 1 Call : colour (granny_smith, green)
(6) 1 Exit : colour (granny_smith, green)
(1) 0 Exit : apple (granny_smith)
X = granny_smith

7.2 The debugging predicates

Although the debugging predicates referred to here are written according to the DEC-10 implementation of Prolog, you should find that with reference to this section and the appropriate User Manual, you will be able to successfully use the debugging facilities on many Prolog interpreters.

In the above two examples you have seen the format of the debugging messages you will receive. In this section we will discuss how to use the standard features of the debugger to assist you in removing bugs from your program.

To switch on the debugging facility the system predicate **debug** is used. To switch the debugger off the predicate **nodebug** is used. You should bear in mind for later in this section that **nodebug** also removes any "spy points" you set in your program. Spy points are a debugging aid that we will discuss shortly. Another predicate you will find useful during extensive debugging sessions is the system predicate **debugging** which will return information about the current state of the debugging facility. For example

> yes
> ?- debugging.
> **Action on unknown procedures: fail**
> **Debug mode is switched on.**
> **Spy-points set on:**
> shape/2
> **Leashing set to half (call, redo).**

Again do not worry about leashing, we will be talking about it soon.

7.2.1 Tracing

Let us suppose that you have written your program, and then you find that it does not work (a common problem!), and you wish to use the debugger to assist in finding the problems. One of the options open to you would be to produce a complete listing of the program flow through all of the procedure boxes called. You can do this using the system predicate **trace**. If the debugger is not already switched on, using **debug** causes the debugger to be activated, and ensures that the next time a procedure box is entered a prompt will be received. At this point a number of control options are available, which will vary according to the system you are using. These may include 'creeping', 'leaping' or 'skipping' through the program.

7.2.2 Creeping

In this mode the interpreter single steps through the program, stopping at the next leashed port (we will talk about leashing shortly) to print out a debugging message and prompt the user. This control is performed using a carriage return command.

7.2.3 Leaping

In this mode the interpreter continues its execution of the program, until a spy point is reached or the program ends. This control is performed using a line feed command.

7.2.4 Skipping

This control is valid only at **CALL** and **REDO** ports. It causes the interpreter to perform the execution of the procedure within the box being entered, without producing any debugging messages or user prompts. The user is prompted again when the procedure is exited or failed. The control is performed using the escape command. When a trace is performed the debugger will output to indicate that a skip was performed when the user was given a chance to interact at one of the ports of a given procedure box. For example, the message could be of the form

> **(13) 1 Exit : colour (granny_smith, green).**

7.2.5 Disabling the trace facility

To disable the trace facility the predicate **notrace** is used. Notice that the predicate **trace** can be used part way through a program, by interrupting the program (using ^C). However if information about the program flow before trace is called is required, the debug mode must have been on from the start of the program execution or the information will be lost.

7.2.6 Leashing

Now that you are able to set up exhaustive tracing using the **trace** predicate, you will probably want to alter the ports at which you are prompted for action. As we have mentioned before, this is done by leashing the ports you wish to be prompted at. The predicate **leash (X)** is used to alter the degree of leashing on all procedure boxes. The variable **X** may be an integer in the range 0 to 15 or a description of the leashing (for example full, half etc.). The integers and corresponding description, if any, are given below along with their effect on the leashing of the procedure boxes.

PROMPT ON

DESCRIPTION	X	CALL	EXIT	REDO	FAIL
off	0	no	no	no	no
	1	no	no	no	yes
	2	no	no	yes	no
	3	no	no	yes	yes
	4	no	yes	no	no
	5	no	yes	no	yes
	6	no	yes	yes	no
	7	no	yes	yes	yes
loose	8	yes	no	no	no
	9	yes	no	no	yes
half	10	yes	no	yes	no
tight	11	yes	no	yes	yes
	12	yes	yes	no	no
	13	yes	yes	no	yes
	14	yes	yes	yes	no
full	15	yes	yes	yes	yes

Thus if we wish to obtain a prompt on only the **CALL** port of a procedure box we could use either

leash (loose).   or   **leash (8).**

The default setting for leash is usually half, that is prompts on **CALL** and **REDO**.

7.2.7 *Spy points*

Clearly using the trace facility will be very useful if small sections of your program are to be debugged, or you have only a small program. However, for large programs this method of debugging would be extremely time consuming and complicated. A higher level of debugging is available which allows you to look at the control flow through certain procedures. This is done by setting 'spy points' on the procedures you are interested in. Placing a spy point on a procedure causes a debugging message and a prompt to appear when control passes into a procedure box with a spy point placed on it. The spy points are placed using the system predicate **spy (X)**, where **X** is the procedure of interest. The variable **X** may be of the form

<atom>   or   <atom>/<arity>

where the arity is the number of arguments the particular predicate has. For example, suppose that we had the following program in the knowledge base

sharp (X) :–knife (X).
sharp:–citrus_fruit.

Then the declarations **spy (sharp/1).**, **spy (sharp/∅).** and **spy (sharp).** would have the following effects

spy (sharp/1).   would place a spy point on **sharp (X)**
spy (sharp/∅).   would place a spy point on **sharp**
spy (sharp).   would place a spy point on both **sharp** and **sharp (X)**

Thus specifying the predicate without an arity places spy points on all procedures of that name, regardless of the arity.

To remove spy points from particular procedures the predicate **nospy (X)** can be used. For example

nospy (sharp/1).

However if you wish to remove all spy points an easier method is to use the predicate **nodebug**. Placing spy points on a procedure causes the prompt ** to appear on the output when tracing the program flow to indicate that a spy point is placed on that particular procedure. For example

** (3) 1 Call : shape (victoria_plum, round) ?

If the procedure has a spy point placed on it and if a skip had been performed on the previous occasion when control was exercised at the port of that procedure box, the trace message would be preceded by the symbols *>. An example is shown below

*> (3) 1 Fail : shape (victoria_plum, round).

8 Case Studies

In this chapter we present two case studies. They are designed to expand upon some of the techniques we have used throughout the book. The examples are relatively simple but could be expanded if desired.

Case study 1

This case study is a package that acts as an insurance quote advice system, and was developed using PROLOG-1 running on an IBM PC. The program is designed to provide the USER with all possible quotes that match his specification. The

'DATA.PRO' — Contains all the output responses, insurance company details, and car details.

'UTIL.PRO' — Contains a number of utility procedures used by the main program 'CONT.PRO.'

'CONT.PRO' — The controlling program. It is used to calculate the quote from the user specification.

The listings for the files are given below. Notice that anything enclosed as shown below is treated as a comment. Thus

/* This is a comment ! */

is treated as a comment.

'DATA.PRO'

/* USER PROMPTS */
/* The lists contained in the argument of the predicate 'resp' are output to the screen using the screen predicate defined in the file UTIL.PRO */

resp (∅, ['

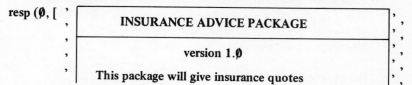

> '   for cars to be insured in the U.K. only   ', '
> '   ', '
> '   Before the clients insurance premium can   ', '
> '   be calculated some details are required.   ', '
> '   ', '
> '   PLEASE ANSWER IN THE MANNER INDICATED   ', '
]).   , '
                                                                             , '

resp (1, [' ',
           ' Please enter the model of the clients car',
           ' Enclose your answer in single quotes.   ']).

resp (2, [' ',
           ' Please enter the engine size in c.c. ']).

resp (3, [' ',
           ' Please enter the date of manufacture ']).

resp (4, [' ',
           ' Give the clients surname and initials',
           ' Enclose your answer in single quotes']).

resp (5, [' ',
           ' Give the clients address ',
           ' Enclose your answer in single quotes']).

resp (6, [' ',
           ' List any convictions according to the codes given ',
           ' ',
           ' Drink Driving . . . . d',
           ' ',
           ' Dangerous driving . . . . dd',
           ' ',
           ' Speeding . . . . .s',
           ' Enter as a list']).

resp (7, [' ',
           ' What is the clients age ']).

resp (8, [' ',
           ' What type of insurance',
           ' ',
           'Third party fire and theft . . . . tpft',

```
                      ' ',
                      ' Full comprehensive . . . . . . . . . . . . .fcomp']).

resp (9, [  ' ',
            ' Please enter any extras according to the ',
            ' following codes',
            ' ',
            ' Protected Policy (fcomp only) . . . . . p ',
            ' ',
            ' Windscreen Insurance . . . . . . . . . . . .w ',
            ' ',
            ' Radio/Cassette insurance . . . . . . . . . r ',
            ' ',
            ' Enter as a list ']).

resp (10,[ ' What is the clients no claims bonus in %']).


   /*Car Data : All the clauses are of the form
               car_grp (CAR TYPE, ENGINE SIZE, INS GROUP)*/
   car_grp ('ford cortina', 2000, 5).
   car_grp ('mini metro', 1300, 3).
   car_grp ('mini metro', 1100, 2).
   car_grp ('M.G. metro', 1300, 4).


   /* Basic premium data : All clauses take the form
          bas_prem (GROUP, COST, COMPANY, TYPE) */
   bas_prem (2,100, 'Cheap Insurance P.L.C.', tpft).
   bas_prem (2,250, 'Pricey Insurance', fcomp).
   bas_prem (2,150, 'Cheap Insurance P.L.C.', fcomp).
   bas_prem (3,349, 'Cheap Insurance P.L.C.', fcomp).
   bas_prem (3,245, 'Cheap Insurance P.L.C.', tpft).
   bas_prem (3,400, 'Pricey Insurance', fcomp).
   bas_prem (3,275), 'Pricey Insurance', tpft).

 /* Company loadings : All clauses are of the form
           loading (COMPANY, TYPE' [[CODES, LOADINGS]]) */
   loading ('Pricey Insurance', tpft, [[d, 300], [s,45], [dd,50]]).
   loading ('Pricey Insurance', fcomp, [[d, 350], [s, 45], [dd, 50]]).
   loading ('Cheap Insurance P.L.C.', tpft, [[d, 400], [s, 30],
      [dd, 80]]).

 /* Costs for Extras*/
   extras ('Pricey Insurance', fcomp, [[p,25], [w,25], [r,30]]).
   extras ('Pricey Insurance', tpft, [[r,30], [w,35]]).
   extras ('Cheap Insurance P.L.C.', fcomp, [[p,25], [w,35],
      Cr,20]]).
```

extras ('Cheap Insurance P.L.C.', tpft, [[r,25], [w,35]]).

```
/* FIND LOADINGS AND EXTRAS */
    calc_load (Options, Data, Results) :-
            calc_load (Options, Data, Ø, Result).
    calc_load ([],_, N, N).
    calc_load ([Option¦Rest], Data, N, Total) :-
            entry (Option, Data, Value),
            Sum is N + Value,
            calc_load (Rest, Data, Sum, Total).

    entry (H, [[H, Y]¦_], Y) :- !.

    entry (H, [_¦T], P) :- entry (H, T, P).

/* FIND THE LENGTH OF A LIST */
    length (X, J) :- flen (X, J, Ø),
    flen ([], Y, Y).
    flen ([H¦T], Y, Z) :- P is Z + 1,
                         flen (T, Y, P).

/* INPUT OUTPUT PROCEDURE */
    ipout (resp (R, X), Y):-call (resp (R, X)),
                           screen (X),
                           nl,
                           write ('¦:'),
                           read (Y).
    screen ([]): -!.
    screen ([H¦T]) :- write (H),
                      nl,
                      screen (T).
```

```
/* READ IN DATA FILE AND UTILITY PROCEDURES */
```

/*To begin the program the user must type go. which causes Prolog to consult the data and utility files */

```
    go:- consult ('data.pro'),
         consult ('until.pro'),
         start.

/* OUTPUT TITLE AND GET USER SPECIFICATION FOR QUOTES */
    start:- resp (Ø, X),
```

```
            screen (X),
            get_car (Data),
            comput (Data).


/* GET CAR DETAILS*/
    get_car (data_struc (A, B)) :- find_car_det (A),
                                    find_driver_det (B).
    find_car_det (car_det (Car, Eng, Cage)) :-
                            ipout (resp (1, X), Car),
                            ipout (resp (2, X1), Eng),
                            ipout (resp (3, X2), Cage).


/* GET DRIVER DETAILS*/
    find_driver_det (driver_det (Driver, Addr, Conv, Age)) :-
                            ipout (resp (4, X), Driver),
                            ipout (resp (5, X1), Addr),
                            ipout (resp (6, X2), Conv),
                            ipout (resp (7, X3), Age).
```

/* COMPUTE INSURANCE QUOTE */

/* The information input by the user is obtained using car_det and details. The
insurance group of the car specified is then found by car_grp. The type of
insurance, any extras and the current no claims bonus are then obtained.
The cut prevents any of the information being requested again, and the cost of
the insurance is computed using the details given and the information on the
various policies contained in the database. Note that fix is a system predicate
to truncate a real number to an integer.*/

```
    compute (data_struc (A, B)) :-
                arg (1, A, Car),
                arg (2, A, Eng),
                car_grp (Car, Eng, Group),
                ipout (resp (8, X), Type),
                ipout (resp (9, X1), Extr),
                ipout (resp (10, X2), Ncb).
                !,
                base_prem (Group, Prem, Comp, Type),
                C = ins_det (Group, Prem, Comp, Type),
                D = extradet (Extr, Ncb),
                prices (A, B, C, D),
                write (' Another Quote y/n : '),
                read (Res),
                Res = n.
```

/* CALCULATE PRICES OF AVAILABLE POLICIES */

```
prices (A, B, C, D) :-
    A = car_det (Car, Eng, Cage),
    B = driver_det (Driver, Addr, Conv, Age),
    C = ins_det (Group, Prem, Comp, Type),
    D = extradet (Extr, Ncb),
                loading (Comp, Type, Load),
                calc_load (Conv, Load, Y),

length (Conv, J),
Loading is fix (Prem*(Y/(J*1ØØ))),
find_xtra (Extra_cost, Type, Comp, Prem, Extr),
discounts (Dis, Cage, Age, E),
cdis (Dis, Prem, E, N),
outp (Driver, Addr, Car, Eng, Cage, Age, Group,
      Comp, Type, Prem, Loading, Extra_cost, N, Ncb),
nl,
nl,
!.
```

/* FIND EXTRAS REQUIRED AND THEIR COST*/

```
find_xtra (B, Type, Comp, Prem, Ext):-
            extras (Comp, Type, Xtra),
            calc_load (Ext, Xtra, Y),
            length (Ext, H),
            B is fix (Prem*(Y/(H*1ØØ))).
```

/* CALCULATE DISCOUNTS */

```
discounts (Dis, Cage, Age, E) :-
            disc (Cage, V, S),
            disca (Age, U, P),
            Dis is U + V,
            Q is S + P,
            ((Q = Ø, E = 1, !); E = Q)
```

/*Discount due to car age*/
```
disc (Cage, 10, 1) :- 1985-Cage> =1Ø,
                        !.

disc (_, Ø, Ø).
```
/*Discount due to age of the driver*/
```
disca (Age, 25, 1) :- Age> = 25,
                        !.

disca (_, Ø, Ø).
```
/*Calculate the reduction in costs due to the discounts*/
```
cdis (Dis, Prem, E, N) :- N is fix (Prem* (Dis/(E*1ØØ))).
```

```
/* OUTPUT FORMATTING */
    outp (Driver, Addr, Car, Eng, Cage, Age, Group, Type, Prem, Loading,
        B, N, Ncb) :-
        write ('                                    Insurance Quotation'), nl,
        write (' Drivers Name . . . . . . . . . . . . . .'), write (Driver), nl,
        write (' Drivers Age . . . . . . . . . . . . . .'), write (Age), nl,
        write (' Address . . . . . . . . . . . . . . . . . .'), write (Addr), nl,
        write (' Insurance Company . . . . . . . . '), write (Comp), nl,
        write (' Insurance Type . . . . . . . . . . . .'), write (Type), nl,
        write (' Vehicle Type . . . . . . . . . . . . '), write (Car),
        tab (2),
        write (Eng), nl,
        write (' Date of Manufacture . . . . . . . '), write (Cage), nl,
        write (' Insurance Group . . . . . . . . . . .'), wrige (Group), nl,
        write (' Basic Premium . . . . . . . . . . . .'), write (Prem), nl,
        write (' Extras Requested . . . . . . . . . .'), write (B), nl,[
        write (' Loadings . . . . . . . . . . . . . . . .'), write (Loading), nl,
        write (' Discounts . . . . . . . . . . . . . . . .'), write (N), nl,
        write (' No Claims Bonus . . . . . . . . . . '), write (Ncb),
        write (' %'), nl,
        Cost is fix ((Prem + B + Loading − N∗(Ncb/100))),
        write (' Amount Payable is . . . . . . . . '), write (Cost), nl.
```

Case study 2

This is a case study that demonstrates how the grammar rule notation of Prolog can be used to construct a small system designed to classify different types of sentences. The program is written as two files, **converse. pl** and **vocab. pl**.

'CONVERSE. PL'

/* This program uses the high level grammar syntax of Prolog to build a natural language processor*/
/* The program was written using Quintus Prolog */

/* 1. Read a sentence and transform it into a list of words */

```
read_sentence (S) :- tab (10),
                write (':'),
                get (C),
                words (C, S).

words (C, [P|Ps]) :- letter (C),
                word (C, c1, L),
                name (P, L),
                words (C1, Ps).
```

```
words (44, [',' Ps]) :- get (C1),
                        words (C1, Ps).
words (45, ['-' Ps]) :- get (C1),
                        words (C1, Ps).
words (59, [';' Ps]) :-  get (C1),
                        words (C1, Ps).
words (63, ['?']).
words (46, ['.']).
words (_,P) :- get (C),
                words (C, P).

words(C, C1, [C¦Cs]) :- get∅(C2),
                        (letter (C2), word (C2, C1, Cs); C1=C2, Cs=[ ]).

letter (32)   :- !,fail.     /* space           */
letter (39)   :- !,fail.     /* quote '          */
letter (34)   :- !,fail.     /* quote "          */
letter (63)   :- !,fail.     /*    ?             */
letter (59)   :- !,fail.     /*    ;             */
letter (45)   :- !,fail.     /* hyphen           */
letter (46)   :- !,fail.     /* stop             */
letter (33)   :- !,fail.     /*    !             */
letter (44)   :- !,fail.     /* comma            */
letter (1∅)   :- !,fail.     /* line feed        */
letter (13)   :- !,fail.     /* carriage return  */
letter (_).                  /* default          */
```

[Authors' note 1. The above section of code is taken from *How to solve it with Prolog* (Helder Coelho, Jose Carlos Cotta and Luis Moniz Pereira, Laboratorio Nacional de Engenharia Civil, Lisboa, Portugal). The book contains many practical case studies of Prolog applications and is highly recommended. The effect of the code is to allow a sentence to be input in normal prose and to be transformed into the much more convenient data structure of a list. For example

```
read_sentence (S).
            :the man and the woman understand
prolog
    S = [the, man, and, the, woman, understand, prolog,'.']
```

As an interesting exercise you might care to attempt to write your own routine to accomplish the same thing.]

```
/* 2. Definition of sentence and phrase structure */
sentence ⟶ noun_phrase, verb_phrase, terminator.
```

sentence ⟶ question.
sentence ⟶ imperative.
noun_phrase ⟶ determiner, noun, extension.
extension ⟶ conjunction, noun_phrase.
extension ⟶ disjunction, noun_phrase.
extension ⟶ [ ].
verb_phrase ⟶ verb, noun_phrase.
verb_phrase ⟶ verb, adverb.
question ⟶ interrogative, noun_phrase, verb_phrase, ['?'].
imperative ⟶ noun, separator, verb_phrase, ['!'].

[Authors' note 2. Here the grammar syntax is used in a straightforward way to describe the general structure of the types of statements that the program will recognise. For instance, the basic form of a sentence is declared to be a noun phrase followed by a verb phrase and ending with a terminator (full stop, question mark or exclamation). As you can see, components of the sentence are then further broken down. **The empty list signifies that a grammar component is not essential to the sentence.**]

```
/* 3. The interactive program */
start_up :- consult ('vocab. pl').

talk :- tab (20),
        write ('enter sentence for validation'), nl, nl,
        read_sentence (S),!,
        phrase (sentence, S),
        nl, nl, tab (20),
        write ('I understand the sentence:'),
        nl, nl, tabl (20), write ('"')
        relay_sentence (S),
        write ('"'),
        classify (S).

classify (S) :-  phrase (question, S),
                 nl, nl, tab (20), write ('it is a question').

classify (S) :-  phrase (imperative, S),
                 nl, nl, tab (20),
                 write ('it is an imperative instruction').

classify (S) :-  nl, nl, tab (20),
                 write ('it is an instructive sentence').

relay_sentence (S) :- word_in (W, S), write (W), write (' '), fail.

relay_sentence (_).
```

word_in (W, [W _]).
word_in (W, [_ T]) :- word_in (W, T).

[Authors' note 3. The interactive program works as follows.
First the system is invoked by the **talk** instruction which produces a prompt
and then requires a sentence to be input. Valid sentences (according to the
grammar and vocabulary rules defined by the program) are then further
classified and an appropriate text message is generated to confirm that the
program recognises the sentence.]

VOCAB.PL

separator ⟶ [' , '].
separator ⟶ [' – '].
separator ⟶ [' ; '].

terminator ⟶ [' . '].
terminator ⟶ [' ? '].
terminator ⟶ [' ! '].

determiner ⟶ [a].
determiner ⟶ [an].
determiner ⟶ [the].
determiner ⟶ [].

conjunction ⟶ [and].

disjunction ⟶ [or].

noun ⟶ [man].
noun ⟶ [woman].
noun ⟶ [child].
noun ⟶ [boy].
noun ⟶ [girl].
noun ⟶ [word].
noun ⟶ [sentence].
noun ⟶ [computer].
noun ⟶ [system].
noun ⟶ [program].
noun ⟶ [prolog].

interrogative ⟶ [does].
interrogative ⟶ [can].
interrogative ⟶ [will].

interrogative ⟶ [should].
interrogative ⟶ [could].

verb ⟶ [says].
verb ⟶ [speaks].
verb ⟶ [speaks, to].
verb ⟶ [speak].
verb ⟶ [speak, to].
verb ⟶ [say].
verb ⟶ [tell].
verb ⟶ [read].
verb ⟶ [recognise].
verb ⟶ [respond, to].
verb ⟶ [understand].
verb ⟶ [repeat].

adverb ⟶ [well].
adverb ⟶ [badly].

[Authors' note 4. A very small vocabulary is defined to the system, adequate only to demonstrate that the program does in fact work as it should. There are better and more sophisticated ways of using the grammar syntax which would need to be employed in the development of a more powerful system. However this small example should give an idea of how Prolog can be used for this type of application. A suggested case study is to take an area wherein the 'domain of knowledge' is small and easily stated and to write a natural language system which can recognise statements and answer simple questions about the domain. By doing so it is possible not only to learn more about the use of Prolog but also about some of the problems associated with interactive and expert system development.]

Appendix 1: Prolog-1 (Version 2)

This software is available from Expert Systems International Ltd. It is available for machines which run under MS-DOS, CP/M-86, CP/M-80 VMS, RSX-11M and RT-11 operating systems. In this appendix we outline the operation of the Prolog interpreter on the IBM PC, and point out the major differences and similarities between this version of Prolog and that supplied on the DEC-10 implementation we have used to describe Prolog throughout the book.

This appendix does not represent a complete description of all the facilities of PROLOG-1, nor is it intended that it should. It is hoped that this short section will give the reader a 'flavour' of the language, for possible future investigation. A complete description of the language package is given in the Reference Manual accompanying the software.

Using the interpreter

There are two mechanisms for entering PROLOG-1. The first is to invoke the top level interpreter PROLOG86, the second is to use the interpreter with the system clause editor PROLED86.

PROLOG86

Invoking this interpreter enables you to read in text files using the system predicates **consult (X)** and **reconsult (X)** as described previously in the book.

PROLED86

This interpreter contains a system clause editor. The clause editor provides facilities for saving and loading files that are distinct from **consult (X)** and **reconsult (X)**. For a complete description of the editor facilities and commands the reader is referred to the User Manual. However it is worthwhile noticing that although it is possible to use the predicates **consult (X)** and **reconsult (X)**, the clauses entered by this method cannot be modified using the clause editor, but you may run the program. To have the option of modifying clauses while in PROLED86 you must have entered, saved and loaded the file of clauses while in PROLED86.

PROLOG-1 *terms*

As we have mentioned earlier a Prolog term may be a constant (atom or number), variable or structure. In PROLOG-1 atoms, variables and structures may be written in the way they have been written throughout this text. However numbers are slightly different. Previously we stated that Prolog supported only integers, but PROLOG-1 supports both integer and real numbers. An integer is a number in the range 0 to 16383 (notice, positive integers only).

A real number may be a signed or unsigned sequence of digits separated by a decimal point, and optionally followed by an exponent (designated by an E). Some examples are given below.

12E-5	**1234E5**	**1.0**	**0.01**	**15.8**	**1.9E+10**
1.9E10	**−4.10**	**−4.10E−10**			

Operators

The specification of operators is performed as mentioned in chapter 6. However notice that the operator precedence range is 1 to 255.

System predicates

The following built in predicates perform as described earlier in the text.

arg (X, Y, Z).	assert (X).	asserta (X).	assertz (X).
atom (X).	atomic (X).	call (X).	consult (X).
debugging.	display (X).	fail.	functor (X, Y, Z).
get (X).	get 0 (X).	halt.	integer (X).
name (X, Y).	nl.	nodebug.	nonvar (X).
nospy (X).	op (X, Y, Z).	print (X).	put (X).
read (X).	reconsult (X).	repeat.	retract (X).
see (X).	seeing (X).	seen (X).	skip (X).
spy (X).	tab (X).	tell (X).	telling (X).
told (X).	trace.	true.	var (X).
write (X).	writeq (X).	X = . . Y.	X = Y.
X==Y.	X\ = Y.	X\==Y.	

The following predicates are not present on the DEC-10 implementation and are listed below together with a brief description of their function.

real (X) — tests to see if **X** is a real number.

numeric (X) — tests to see if **X** is a real number or an integer.

retractall (X) — removes all predicates from the database with name and arity **X**.

not (X) — performs negation. This predicate acts in the same way as \+(X) defined in the chapter on system predicates.

Arithmetic

The following arithmetic operators perform functions as previously described.

X<Y.   X>Y.   X=:=Y.   X=<Y.   X=\=Y.
X>=Y.   X is Y.

You will notice that the above operators are the set of comparison and assignment terms discussed previously. As already mentioned, the PROLOG-1 language supports both real and integer numbers. There are therefore several system predicates provided for, dealing with real numbers as listed below.

float (X)   – gives a floating point version of the integer **X**.
fix (X)   – returns an integer equivalent to **X** truncated toward $\emptyset$.
real_round (X) – rounds **X** to a real number, away from $\emptyset$.
truncate (X)   – returns a real number equivalent to **X** truncated toward $\emptyset$.

Addition, multiplication and subtraction

These operations are indicated by the same operators mentioned in the chapter on arithmetic. However the number type of the result depends on the operands. Consider the following

X op Y

where X and Y are the operands and **op** is an operator from the set +, −, *.
Then if X and Y are both integer expressions the result will be an integer expression, otherwise the result will be a real number.

Division

Two operators are used for division

The / operator performs real division.
The // operator performs integer divison. Notice that the operands for this operator must be integer types.

The remainder of the integer division of X by Y is given by the expression Y **mod** Y. Again both X and Y are integer.

The PROLOG-1 debug facilities

The tracing facility is enabled and disabled using the predicates **trace** and **notrace** respectively. The tracing messages output are **Goal** when trying to satisy a goal, and **Proved** when that goal has been proved. No messages are output if the goal

fails or if an attempt is made to resatisfy the goal. However a message is output
if the attempt to resatisfy the goal is successful.

Spy points are set and removed from clauses using the predicates **spy (X)** and
nospy (X). The variable X must be a predicate name or a predicate name followed
by an arity enclosed in round brackets. For example, given the following database

> nam(a, b).
> nam (c,d).
> nam (b, h, j).

then a call **spy (nam)** will place spy points on all three clauses in the database,
whereas a call **spy (nam(3))** will place a spy point on the final clause only. The
predicates **debugging** and **nodebug** perform the same function as discussed in
chapter 7.

An example session using the debug facility is outlined below.

> /*Database*/
> fruit (granny_smith).
> shape (victoria_plum, round).
> shape (granny_smith, round).
> colour (victoria_plum, purple).
> colour (granny_smith, green).
> apple (X) :- fruit (X),
>   shape (X, round),
>   colour (X, green).
>
> ?-debugging.
> There are no spy-points set.
>
> yes
> ?- spy (colour).
> Spy-point placed on colour (2).
>
> yes
> ?-apple (X).
> Spy Goal colour (granny_smith, green)
> Spy proved colour (granny_smith, green)
> X = granny_smith
> More (y/n)? n
>
> yes
> ?- trace.
> yes
> ?-apple (X).

Goal apple (_44)
Goal fruit (_44)
Proved fruit (granny_smith)
Goal shape (granny_smith, round)
Proved shape (granny_smith, green)
Spy Goal colour (granny_smith, green)
Spy Proved colour (granny_smith, green)
Proved colour (granny_smith, green)
Proved apple (granny_smith, green)
Proved apple (granny_smith)
X = granny_smith
More (y/n)? n

Input output

The input output facilities provided are an enhanced version of those discussed earlier in the book. As mentioned in the chapter on system predicates, the predicates **read, write, tell** etc. are all included, as well as the predicate **getbyte(x)** which succeeds if X matches with the next byte on the current input stream.

Random file access

PROLOG-1 also permits random file access rather than the serial type access provided by **read, write, get,** and **put**. Random access may be performed on any disc file; the pointer to the file is positioned using the predicates **seek_read (X)** and **seek_write (X)**, where **X** represents the file pointer position in terms of a block number and an offset. Thus a call to **seek_read (1 + 2)** sets the pointer to the second byte of the first block (that is, the 130th byte), of the current input stream. The start of a file is specified by **0 + 0**. The reader is referred to the section on random file access in the User Manual for further information.

Calling external procedures

External procedures may be called using the **external_code** predicate. The predicate has three arguments: an operation number in the range 0 to 255, an input parameter list and an output list. The input and output parameter lists may contain up to 8 parameters. An example is given below

status (A, B, C) :- external_code (1, [A], [B, C]).

The call to **status (A, B, C)** now corresponds to a call to the external section of machine code, passing the parameter assigned to the variable **A**, and receiving the parameters **B** and **C**.

The User Manual contains full details on setting up calls to external code.

Appendix 2: Quintus Prolog (Version 1.2)

Quintus Prolog is an advanced implementation of the language. The objectives of its designers (David Warren, Lawrence Byrd, Bill Kornfeld and Fernando Pereira) were to produce a version of the language which would offer fast execution speeds as well as the capability to communicate with other software. The software is available from Artificial Intelligence Ltd and runs under UNIX and VMS operating systems on the VAX-11 and SUN-2 hardware systems. All the examples in this book (based as you know on DEC Prolog) will run under Quintus Prolog because DEC Prolog is a compatible subset of Quintus Prolog. This appendix does not attempt to describe the language in fine detail because a complete description is given in the Reference Manual accompanying the software. However, we will point out the following main features of the Quintus software.

1. The Editor Interface

An interesting feature is the interface to the EMACS editor, which may be accessed by the commands

    prolog +
    or prolog + <file-to-be-edited>

in response to the UNIX prompt. These commands cause EMACS to run with two windows: file-to-be-edited if given will appear in the upper window while Prolog will run in the lower window. Thus it is possible to execute code and see code at the same time. It is possible to access Prolog in much the same way as you would without the EMACS editor interface, since the Prolog window is still an edit buffer. Full details of the commands available are contained in the Reference Manual.

A style checker is also supplied with Quintus Prolog which will warn the user of

(1) single occurrences of named variables in a clause (that is, those not beginning with the underline character)
(2) procedures for which all the clauses are not adjacent in the source file.

2. Entering clauses

Prolog clauses may be entered from text files using either the **consult** or **compile** predicates. However it should be noted that **consult** under Quintus Prolog behaves as **reconsult** would under DEC-10 Prolog. This means that a procedure may not be spread across more than one file unless it is required that clauses of the same name are deleted from the database when a consult is performed. It is also possible to modify the database using assert and retract, as discussed previously.

3. The debugger

The Quintus debugger closely resembles that described previously for DEC-10 Prolog. It provides facilities for single step tracing and selective debugging, using spy points placed on both compiled and interpreted procedures.

The following predicates are available for debugging

trace	— sets a state in which the debugger will start creeping on every goal typed in at the top level.
debug	— sets a state in which the debugger will leap on every goal typed in at the top level.
notrace	— turns the debugger off.
spy	— sets required spy points.
nospyall	— removes all spy points. Note that turning the debugger off will not remove the set spy points.

The debugger options + and − are available to set and remove spy points, respectively. The option = may be used to display the current debugging information.

Leashing

It is possible to leash the ports, by specifying the ports to be leashed as a list. For example, the command

leash ([ ]).

removes all leashing, causing an exhaustive trace upon creeping. The command

leash ([call, redo]).

places leashes on the call and redo ports.

4. Arithmetic

Quintus Prolog offers both floating point and integer arithmetic. A floating
point number is written as a signed decimal fraction with a decimal point, at
least one digit before and after the decimal point and an optional base ten
exponent. Some examples are given below

$$0.0 \quad -1.0 \quad 0.54 \quad 1000.0 \quad 1.0e6 \quad 12.345678e-12$$

Arithmetic operators

Addition, subtraction and multiplication have the operators +, −, and * respectively for both integer and floating point arithmetic. Integer division is
performed by the // operator, the result being an integer type. Floating point
division is performed using the / operator; the result is a floating point number.

System predicates for testing terms

The following predicates apply

integer (X) — Truncates **X** to an integer, or returns **X** if **X** is an integer.
float (X) — Results in **X** if **X** is a floating point number, or if **X** is an
                integer the result is the floating point equivalent.
number (X)— Succeeds if **X** is instantiated to either an integer or a floating
                point number; if not it fails.

There are other predicates used for the testing of terms but in the main they
are compatible with the DEC-10 system.

Input/output

As with the systems discussed before, it is possible to conduct input and
output on the USER or the current stream. The predicates for use on these
streams are compatible with those described throughout the book. However
it is also possible to use the predicates for input and output with reference to
a specific stream. This facility includes more advanced file handling predicates
as well as input and output predicates which can be related to specific streams.
For example, **write (X, S)** causes output to the stream identified by **S**.

The interface to C

This is a feature that is of great importance if Prolog is to be used a component
in the production of large and sophisticated systems. We cannot go into detail
in this appendix since the appropriate place for such material is within the

user specification for Quintus Prolog. However the process of interfacing
Prolog with other software facilities is addressed by the provision of simple
interfaces under UNIX and VMS. Examples of applications that have been developed using this technique include the following: incorporation of complex
mathematical routines within Prolog programs (achieved by interfacing with
the C mathematics library), incorporation of graphics displays controlled by
Prolog programs, and use of external database management systems to provide
mass data driving for Prolog programs.

Applications such as the ones described above are undoubtedly outside the
scope of any text-book about the Prolog language *per se* but we mention them
in order to offer the reader some perspective on how the language may be used
in more advanced processing environments.

The Quintus interpreter and compiler

We have already mentioned the EMACS controlled program development
environment. Within this environment, the user screen is split into two sections
— one is used for code development, the other for program execution. Movement
between the two windows is achieved by the command sequence CTRL X ∅.

Quintus Prolog offers a range of interpreter and compiler options as
follows. For both interpreter and compiler level execution, it is possible to select
a complete buffer area (that is, all the code in a window), a marked region of
the buffer or an individual procedure to interpret/compile. Furthermore,
interpreted and compiled code will run quite freely together — thus, if
one procedure of a program is faulty it is necessary only to debug that procedure and re-interpret or compile it without having to interpret or compile the
whole program again.

Generally speaking, the intention is that the interpreter should be used for
program development and the compiler for live running where it is likely that
execution speed will be a major priority. The interperter is invoked by the
command sequence **ESC i** and the compiler by the command sequence **ESC k**
followed by the appropriate selection of buffer, region or procedure.
Alternatively, they may be invoked by the system predicates **consult** and **compile**. For example

    consult ('Prog_file1.pro').

causes the named file to be interpreted and

    compile ('Prog_file2').

causes the named file to be compiled.

It should be noted that although the interpreter offers only the average
performance (in terms of code execution speed) associated with program

development, the compiler when invoked provides fast execution speeds.

Another interesting feature of this implementation is the provision of a 'break' in program execution — this allows the programmer to alter faulty code during the run of a program. In order to do so, a 'break' can be commanded when an error occurs, the code causing the error being corrected and re-interpreted or recompiled and the program run recommenced with the corrected code incorporated in the program. This feature is particularly useful for debugging large and complex programs.

A comprehensive description of interpreter and compiler facilities appears in the documentation accompanying the software.

Appendix 3: A List of ASCII Characters and their Codes

Character	Code
space	32
!	33
"	34
#	35
$	36
%	37
&	38
'	39
(	40
)	41
*	42
+	43
,	44
-	45
.	46
/	47
0-9	48-57
:	58
;	59
<	60
=	61
>	62
?	63
@	64
A-Z	65-90
[	91
\	92
]	93
^	94
_	95
`	96
a-z	97-122
{	123
		124
}	125
~	126

Index

abolish   72
addition   32
ancestors   74
arg   75
arguments   17
arithmetic   31
arity   17
assert   61
asserta   61
assertions   1
assertz   61
atom   75
atomic   75
atoms   20

backtracking   27, 29
blank variable   22

call   76
clauses   17, 19
comments   90
consult   72
cut   36

debugging   83
display   71
division   33

entry   50
equality   34

fail   63
functor   75

get   58
get0   58
goals   18
grammar rules   80

head   45

inequality   35

inference   5, 11
integer   75
is   32

knowledge base   7

leash   87
length   76
lists   45, 47

multiplication   33

name   60
negation   65
nl   57
nonvar   75
nospy   89
notrace   87

operators   33, 37

pattern matching   24
phrase   81
predicates   17
put

read   54
reconsult   72
recursion   37, 40
repeat   64
retract   62
rules   4, 11

search   24, 28
spy   88
structures   19
subtraction   33
syntax   2, 12
system predicates   57

tab   69
tail   45

trace   87
true   64
tty predicates   70

var   74
variables   4

write   55
writeq   71

\+   66
=..   75
==   76
\==   77

=   77
\=   77
;   14
_ (underline)   14
+   32
−   33
*   33
/   33
=:=   34
>   34
>=   34
<   35
=<   35
¦   47